# Paul Kalmbach 10-24-1897 Knadau, Krasnodar, Russia to 8-12-1981 Seattle, WA, USA

Get past the extremes and innocence
of a wild but simple life in a Russian village, rivers
flush with every fish, young children thinking
nothing of tying lizard tails together at play, amidst
cossacks on horseback in bear caps returning from
the hunt rife with wolf pelts, and feel astounding
adventures, in this true story, of a German-Russian
boy growing up near Krasnodar,
immediately preceding the Bolshevik Revolution.

Devour this autobiography, available for the first time on
paperback, of brave and lucky Paul, who
escaped by himself at sixteen, on a ship bound for
North America, initially joining cousins in Calgary,
Canada, attending Redfield College Academy and
Seminary in South Dakota; then York College in
Nebraska. Fulfilling his Mother's wish to become a
Congregational Minister, and later Real Estate
Agent, surviving college work, dock work and
Chicago's 1920's Mob Streets, and managing to
send money back to his family in Russia, he created
his own family, only to discover what happened to
those who tried to remain in his beloved Caucasus.

Sorrow and heartbreak, love and inspiration,
strength, shock and excitement fill your spirit in
this amazingly, unique peek into the vivid
memories of the man who visited this thrilling,
fascinating and uplifting experience --
always cherishing his destiny of becoming American.

**FOR THE FIRST TIME ON PAPERBACK
AUTHOR'S WORDS UNCHANGED
ACTUAL HISTORIC PHOTOS ADDED BY GRANDAUGHTER**

**Cover Photo Tamara Lorenz Hampton**

# AN ANGEL ON MY SHOULDER

## by
## PAUL KALMBACH

Lulu Press, Inc. * Raleigh, NC

*Copyright © 2013 Tamara K. Hampton*
All Rights Reserved
Tamara Hampton Publishing
Third Revision
*Originally publication hardcover 1977 by Dorrance & Company*
Printed in the United States of America
ISBN 978-0-578-12452-0

*To my family*

# CONTENTS

|     | Intro | ix |
| --- | --- | --- |
|     | Preface | 1 |
| 1.  | *Family Background* | 4 |
| 2.  | *Early Years in Dolinowka* | 8 |
| 3.  | *Adventurous Stanitza Life* | 21 |
| 4.  | *A Tragic Event Brings Sorrow* | 64 |
| 5.  | *The German Village of Blumenfeld* | 71 |
| 6.  | *Back To Dolinowka* | 79 |
| 7.  | *Exciting City Life* | 94 |
| 8.  | *America, Here I Come!* | 122 |
| 9.  | *Public School in Canada* | 149 |
| 10. | *Redfield College* | 165 |
| 11. | *World War I Years* | 183 |
| 12. | *Theology* | 191 |
| 13. | *Chicago and Destiny* | 210 |
| 14. | *Back to Church and College* | 222 |
| 15. | *My First Parish* | 234 |
| 16. | *Odessa, Washington* | 250 |
| 17. | *Hastings, Nebraska* | 266 |
| 18. | *Biola, California* | 281 |
| 19. | *War Years in Portland, Oregon* | 294 |
| 20. | *The Nephew Has Arrived* | 329 |
| 21. | *Life in Its Greatest Dimension* | 346 |

## INTRODUCTION
## BY TAMARA LORENZ HAMPTON

This book is being made made available in entirety, reasonably, so the story is not forgotten and is known and understandable on a more pervasive basis.

Although names were changed in the original, hardback version by the author for publication; the words of my Grampa Kalmbach, what happened to him before, during and after he escaped Soviet Russia, remain unchanged.

Available for the first time in paperback, the only changes for this second edition, other than this explanation, are: spelling corrections, cover art and additions which include:

1) significant portions of authentic, personal, government documents of the times,

2) a glossary of Russian terms and phrases, and

3) rare, treasured family photos, testaments to a bygone era.

If anything else was changed, my sincere apologies, as it is totally unintentional and purely accidental.

# AN ANGEL
ON MY SHOULDER

# PREFACE

THIS BOOK IS THE STORY OF a fifteen-year-old boy, who one day packed his suitcase with some necessities, tied the red quilt that his mother made for him on top of it, took leave of his family and his beloved Caucasus, and migrated to America.

It was his intention to prepare himself for the ministry and upon completion of his training return to Russia to serve the German-Russian people.

Historical events that followed shortly thereafter destroyed that dream, and he would never hear the rhythm of the *troikas* or see any of his family again.

The First World War and the Russian Revolution that followed caused him to undergo the most excruciating mental torment. He felt himself on a roller coaster of euphoria and despair. As the life in America lifted him up to joy and happiness, the heartbreaking news from home plunged him into the depths of gloom and sorrow. He was living physically in a paradise, while at the same time going through an emotional purgatory.

Despite these soul-scarring events, he kept to his books. Entirely self-supporting, he had to work his way through school.

The persecution suffered by the German-Russian people reached its peak during the Stalin era. This Georgian monster, who did not have a drop of Russian blood in him (the Russians being by nature a kind and friendly people) was motivated by the same kind of insanity that drove the Austrian Adolph Hitler to perpetrate a crime against the Jewish people that will always be a stench in the nostrils of humanity. The German people, who since the reign of Catherine had been the backbone of Russian agriculture, were murdered, dispossessed, and exiled.

Many of my own family were executed or banished from their homes. When the details of these atrocities committed against my family reached me, I was heartbroken. It became increasingly difficult for me to face my congregation without breaking down in tears. I saw no other recourse than to resign from the ministry and try to rebuild my crumbled castle. Through my wonderful family, that eventually became possible, so I can again say I am proud to be an American and happy to be a Christian.

## Chapter 1
## FAMILY BACKGROUND

SINCE MUCH HAS BEEN WRITTEN concerning the history of the German people residing in Russia, it is not my intention to bore the reader with information that is available in any library, but to focus attention on a family that was haunted, persecuted, and almost completely wiped out

Before starting the journey through this Soviet labyrinth of tears and sorrow that will bring to light some of the most fiendish actions taken against my people, it is proper that my immediate ancestors be introduced:

The paternal grandfather, Gottlieb Kalmbach, was a German schoolmaster in the village of Postal, near the city of Odessa. He was by stature a rotund man who would have had to be a foot taller to look grandmother straight in the eye. When seen together they were almost a grotesque couple. She, tall and lean, taking strides as if she were stepping off a building site; and he, almost jogging to keep up. But what grandfather lacked in height he more than made up for in girth. Despite the physical mismatch, they were a happy couple. Grandmother was a young widow and married grandfather, bringing with her a son, George, who in later life became the owner of several flour mills. The firstborn in the family was my father, who, according to tradition, was named after his father. He had two brothers, Jacob and John. Jacob became a talented musician, and John followed his father in the teaching profession. A sister, Kathryn, was married to a wagon manufacturer; and the youngest in the family, Rosina was married to one of the Czar's dragoons.

Now for the distaff side of the family. Mother's maiden name was Sandau. Grandfather Sandau, who was known as a physical giant, lost his life trying to save the life of a worker who had been pinned under a collapsed building scaffold. In lifting the scaffold, he suffered internal injury that caused his death. Mother had a younger brother, John, and a sister, Rosine; both had migrated to America. John had become a farmer in South Dakota, and Rosine had married a German Congregational minister residing in Calgary, Alberta, Canada. The widowed grandmother Sandau married a very wealthy landowner, Johannes Belz. He had been a *shabban* (sheep rancher) in Poland and had driven a large herd of sheep all the way into the Caucasus. As one of the first settlers in the small village of Dolinowka, he was able to acquire enough land to establish a hamlet composed of seven houses on his land away from the village. These houses were occupied by his sharecroppers, over whom he ruled like a feudal lord. He also had holdings in the Tashkent area, which he had acquired by means of a mortgage forfeiture--having financed a wildcat drilling for oil in the Baku area. He was known as the richest and stingiest man in the territory.

Both grandparents migrated to the Caucasus about the same time, pioneering in the village of Dolinowka.

In my family were three boys and two girls: the eldest, John, sister Maria, brother Robert, Paul, and baby sister Rosalia.

## Chapter 2
## EARLY YEARS IN DOLINOWKA

THE VILLAGE OF DOLINOWKA was a small but prosperous community of about forty families. Isolated from other German villages, it was located approximately twenty miles south of the city of Krasnodar. The village was often referred to by the Russians as *Bohaty Nemzy,* "the rich Germans." The nearest Russian community was the *stanitza* Nowevelichevka, with a population of around fifteen thousand, mostly cossacks. The most impressive building in a Russian *stanitza* of thatched or straw roofs was always the church. Its onion-shaped towers could be seen a long way off.

Entering Dolinowka from the north one could see all the way down the street to where the Banur River crossed, at the southern end of the village. The street was flanked on each side by a row of locust trees and was a most impressive sight, especially when they were in full bloom. The perfumed air was intoxicating.

The similarity in the houses was at once apparent. The architectural style was definitely German. The walls were either adobe or brick, most of them with thatched roofs. There was a house that stood out like a mother hen, and that was grandfather Belz's home. It was of Mediterranean architecture, a two-and-a-half-story mansion with tile roof and balcony front and back. The houses were all lined up with one of the gables facing the street with the exception of the Belz home, which faced the street with one side forward. Most homes had only three rooms: a front room occupied by the parents; a family kitchen in the center, where the family spent most of its time; and a back room, serving as the sleeping quarters for the rest of the family. The hired hand slept either in the stable or, as was the case in the Belz yard, in a bunkhouse. There was one other feature, and that was a small door just large enough to enable one to crawl through it into the adjoining horse stable. The purpose of this entry was to enable one to lock or bolt the stable doors from the inside.

The villagers took great pride in the ornate brick walls along the fronts of the properties. They were always uniformly whitewashed. No one dared to neglect the appearance of the walls. Beside the larger gate for vehicular traffic there was a little entrance with a decorative overhead arch to permit foot traffic, especially at night, when the larger gate was closed and locked. Grandfather Belz's courtyard reminded one of an early American fortress of the Old West. As one entered through the small gate, one passed along a well-kept rose garden that could be entered only through the house or a gate, since it, too, was surrounded by a brick wall somewhat lower than the walls along the street. The basement of the house was divided into two levels. Half was the kitchen and dining area where the servants ate. Down a flight of steps was the wine cellar, where huge kegs of wine flanked the walls.

Next to the house, following in a horseshoe pattern, was the ice cellar, then the implements shed and the granary. Then there was an open space between the courtyard and the barns on the other side. Still following the horseshoe around, one would have come to the corral, where the calves were kept; and, continuing, one would come to the cow barn, the horse stable, and the bunkhouse.

The backyard was the place where the thrashing of grain and sunflowers took place. The stacks of straw and hay were put neatly in line. On the other side was a long shed containing the grain feed for the stock.

There was still a second division marked off by a barrier, beyond which was the fruit and berry orchard and beyond that several acres of vineyard.

One inevitable feature found in every yard was the watchdog, usually a vicious animal kept chained. At night the chain would be attached to a pulley that ran on a wire the entire length of the barn. Sometimes in the dark of night, when entering a yard, one could see sparks flying on the wire as the animal darted to and fro. Occasionally a chain dog would break his leash. Immediately the neighbors were notified that a dog was loose and to be on the lookout. Despite this added precaution to guard the stock, horse thieves would often chop passages through the walls and make away with the horses.

As one proceeded down the street to the southern end of the village, one would come to the Banur River, which ran due west. Looking across the river there, one would always see things of interest. The large produce tracts were owned and operated by a Turk. He was therefore named by the villagers the "Cabbage Turk." For irrigating the land with river water he had erected a water wheel which would be turning all day long. The power was supplied by a meek little Mongolian pony that would keep walking the circle with a feedbag dangling over its mouth from morning till night. Every once in a while the silence was broken by the chanting and wailing of the owner as he said his prayers to Allah, no doubt facing towards Mecca.

The river had an abundant stock of fish of almost every kind. And if one so desired, there were always spots where one could find the succulent crayfish in abundance. Walking along the river any time of the year, one could always find fishermen with their boats anchored in the bullrushes along the shore and bamboo fishing poles extended toward the stream. Even in the winter, when there was a thick sheet of ice on the river, which would always last until spring, the ardent fisherman found ways to bring trout and bass to his dinner table. All he had to do was chop a hole in the ice, sprinkle some bran on the water, and drop in a line with a baited hook; and in no time the fisherman, sitting on a little stool or box, would be surrounded by landed fish, jumping and squirming around him.

The villagers made good use of the river. In the summertime, children and young people used it for swimming and diving. Since bathing was done in the nude, mixed groups were not permitted. Little children stayed away from their elders, and young maidens were never molested by curious males. If on occasion someone was reported to have violated this rule, a severe reprimand was sure to follow.

Another event quite often took place whenever a group of cossacks rode through the town. Knowing that they were admired by the youngsters, they almost always put on a show of horsemanship for the benefit of all. Some of the cossacks got to be well known, so that all the boys had their favorite performers.

Aside from wheat and corn raising, the villagers indulged in making wine. The Russians from the surrounding localities would come to the village to stock up on wine. The villagers had a certain routine that they would follow to make the sales, and it was one agreed upon by all. The would-be purchaser was taken on a sampling tour. Strictly according to the Bible, the good wine was sampled first; when the time came, which did not take too long, the would-be buyer was hardly able to tell good wine from buttermilk, and he usually wound up buying the worst wine in stock. These transactions always produced a lot of laughter after the buyers had left the village.

Despite its small size, the village

had a flour mill, a brewery, two grocery stores, a tavern, and a brick factory.

To keep order was the responsibility of the *sodzky* (town marshal) and the s*chultz* (magistrate). The marshal walked the street until late in the evening and later would turn the night watch over to two deputies. These deputies were usually young men of the village, and all had to take their turns serving as night watchmen. They were not permitted to carry guns, but were armed with bayonets attached to hickory clubs. In the morning, before going off duty, they would simply leave the weapons in front of the doors of those next in line, the names of which were given to them by the constable.

The teenagers had the village divided into upper and lower zones. Any boy wishing to see a sweetheart in the opposite zone had to make sure not to be seen or caught.

Whenever it happened that thieves got away with someone's horses, the town cryer was immediately notified. He then walked up and down the street, swinging a bell to get everyone's attention and shouting out the order that all able-bodied men of the village were requested to come, armed, and join the posse. Quite often they were successful in tracking down the abandoned horses, though not often the thieves. Once, when grandfather's horses were stolen, the posse found the horses shackled and grazing outside a nearby Russian stanitza, but there was no way to find out who the thieves were.

Only two Russian families lived in the village. Both were quite wealthy and well liked. One family lived across the street, opposite Belz's house. There were two boys in that family, Gavrilla and Sidor. The younger of the two always insisted on speaking German, and it was hilarious to listen to him. Speaking German with Russian sentence structure was a treat to listen to. For example, here is an experience he related of a bicycle accident that he had had: "Riding bicycle on road I ahead looked and see big hole standing in road, I fast driving not can stop and ---troch! [bingo]--my cycle explode." He never lacked willing ears to listen to him. Gavrilla, the older one, however, was very aloof and often gone for days. He was under suspicion for having been the scout for some of the horse thieves, since quite often after he returned home, someone's horses disappeared. The pressure of suspicion finally made him leave the village and stay away.

The summers were hot. From twelve noon to two o'clock was siesta time. Everybody was either taking a nap or sitting in the shade spinning yarns and entertaining others.

The winters were extremely cold. The heavy snow blanket covering the earth stayed the entire winter season. The only kind of transportation was the sled. It was fun for young and old, especially the children. Everybody turned out for sleigh riding. Even the horses seemed conscious of the fact that it was fun. They would curve their necks and prance and strut as if they were competing with each other. The delightful screaming of the children and the singing of the young people filled the air.

There was always someone in the crowd of drivers that could not resist tying to pass a sled ahead of him. The horses themselves would immediately accept the challenge, and the race would be on. Most of the horses were of Arabian stock, and the villagers tried to outdo each other in having the best. Unfortunately, this happy village life was interrupted for our family when we decided to move elsewhere.

## Chapter 3
## ADVENTUROUS STANITZA LIFE

FATHER WAS PERSUADED TO BUY a flour mill and a vegetable oil processing plant in the Stavropol area. The exact location was in the outskirts of the *stanitza* Kursala, approximately forty miles south of Stavropol. The *stanitza* had a population somewhere in the neighborhood of eighteen to twenty thousand families.

Before we were ready to move, however, tragedy struck. An epidemic of smallpox hit the village, and both my brother Robert and I came down with the sickness. I was fortunate enough to overcome it, but Robert, one and a half years older than I, died.

Father took the death of his little son very hard. He was his favorite, and he never tired of asking, "Whose little boy are you?" And with his jet-black eyes sparkling with delight, the boy always answered, "Daddy's *fatz"* (unable to say *schwarz augiger* ("Daddy's black-eyed one").

Whenever the two of us got into a quarrel, it was always Robert who had to be helped--he was not a fighter. I was considered the bully. With Robert gone, my adversary from then on was my mischievous sister Maria. She was an incurable tease, and that, together with my temper, kept us constantly in hot water.

The day of departure had finally arrived. Several wagons, loaded with household goods and covered with canvas, stood ready to depart. We started for Krasnodar, from where the furniture would be shipped by rail. The trip to the city was, of course, very exciting for my sister and me. Father would make us periodically get off the wagon to stretch our legs. It was fun to run alongside the wagons until we were tired.

At our destination, it was as if we had arrived in a different country altogether. At first the contrast was disappointing. Everybody was either Russian, Georgian, or Armenian. Passing through the *stanitza*, we did not get a glimpse of the mill until we had crossed the river on the opposite side of the village. The sight of the mill made up for our first disappointing impression. There it stood--a two and a half-story structure with a tall brick chimney belching smoke.

As per a prearranged signal, the minute we had crossed the bridge, the steam whistle started to blow and kept it up until we arrived in the courtyard.

It was almost as if we had arrived on a school campus. Besides the mill, there were three residences, a cluster of barns, and a huge granary adjoining the mill. Our house was to one side of the mill; on the other side was the miller's home, and behind the boiler room lived the chief engineer.

The exciting feature for sister and me was the case thrashing outfit that stood in the yard. At harvesttime this machine would be out thrashing the grain for the peasants, but the rest of the time it was a wonderful toy for an adventurous boy and girl.

Grandfather Kalmbach retired from teaching and soon followed us. He and grandmother moved into the home that had had to be vacated by the engineer.

Uncle, in the meantime, had received notice to report for military duty. Father knew how to pull strings to have him assigned to barracks very close by.

Grandfather's job was to weigh in the grain that the peasants brought to the mill, and keep part of the wheat in lieu of payment for grinding their wheat. Every so often the caravan of grain haulers would appear in order to take our grain to the nearest market in Stavropol.

Father had great need of Uncle John. But how could he get him out of the army? He made several trips to visit Uncle John and by coincidence was introduced to the army physician. Since father made friends very easily, he soon had the physician in his pocket. It was agreed that my uncle should fake rheumatism but always show willingness to return to duty. This went on for some time. Uncle would be in the infirmary for a few days, then show that he was ready to go out on the training field, only to succumb to another attack. Finally the physician decided that he was too much of a liability and managed to get him a discharge. The day he came home we all ran out to greet him. Sister and I kept repeating, "The sick soldier has come home!"

It struck us rather strange that Uncle John never again was bothered with rheumatism. He certainly was a great help to father, and it was his job to see to it that the peasants kept to their assigned milling time and did not get out of order. The arrangement was on a first-come-first-serve basis. The sacking of the flour had to be taken care of by the customers themselves.

The area in front of the mill always looked like an open marketplace. Peasants would be sleeping on top of their loaded wagons waiting for their turn at the mill.

Sister and I had unlimited opportunities for adventure and fun. There were Russian windmills studding the countryside. They had to be visited. The owners of these crude contraptions were as a rule Russian and very hospitable. As soon as they had established our identity, they would show us through the mill. There was not too much to see. The operation was simple. There were two large stone disks about eight feet across the surface. These stones were pitted by means of steel chisels, leaving the surface jagged with sharp points. One disk was stationary, and the top one kept rotating, thus crushing the wheat kernels. This produced whole wheat flour, the principle flour used to bake their bread.

We felt quite proud that our mill produced white flour and was much more complicated. Invariably, the owners would invite us into their humble homes and treat us to some *prainiky* (cookies) and *kwass*, a beverage made out of fermented bread crusts and quite a delicious thirst quencher.

Walking to and from these excursions, we always had to walk through a field of thistles. When in bloom, they gave the appearance of an army of soldiers with pink and blue fur caps. I imagined them to be enemy soldiers, and since I was riding a bamboo stick, my steed would get excited and anxious for battle. However, the prancing and strutting had to be done by two skinny legs. Charging in on the enemy, I fancied myself a cossack with sword in hand, swinging and decapitating the adversary left and right. Occasionally, I would hear my sister calling out to me, "Look out! There is one behind you!" And so in every battle there would be a number of headless thistles standing in the field. Life was just one continuous picnic.

Another exciting diversion we had was to tie two lizards together by their tails and let them have a tug-of-war while each of us rooted for our own entry.

Fortunately the snakes around there were of the nonpoisonous variety. Some of them got to be quite large, but they were harmless. One day the coachman, Mittya, killed one and left it lying behind the well. It still looked alive except for its crushed head. Now, no seven-year-old boy worth his salt would leave that snake without making some use of it. First I made sure that no one was in the summer kitchen; then I took the snake and carried it into the kitchen. Carefully pushing the crushed head under the range so it could not be seen, I arranged the rest of the body in such a way that it would indicate that the reptile was alive.

Hiding in a carriage standing not far from the building, I waited. The first one to come from the house towards the kitchen was the maid, Maria. For a minute she stood petrified in the doorway. Suddenly, she managed a bloodcurdling scream, jumped back, and ran into the house, calling mother. This turned out to be more fun than I had anticipated. Mother peeked in and ran for father. Now, I knew that a Saint George had been called into the act. What would he do? Father did not even enter the kitchen, but called out in a loud and clear voice, "Paul, wherever you are, you come out this minute!"

Innocent or guilty, when father called, one could not afford to pretend deafness. Slowly I crawled from the coach to face justice. Fortunately there was still enough boy left in father that his sense of humor outweighed mother's indignation. He pretended to give me a severe lecture, but the twinkle in his eyes assured me that his heart was not in it. He had enjoyed the prank as much as I had. Dragging the reptile out of the kitchen, I had to show some speed, for both mother and the maid came after me.

Sister and I had no other playmates except some Russian children that would occasionally come along with their fathers to the mill. It never took us long to organize some kind of game to include them.

One episode that lingered long in our

memories was a target practice, where we used rotten eggs as hand grenades. Marie had removed all the unfertile eggs from the brood nests and told us to take them far away from the house and smash them. Now, an unfertile egg under a brooding hen or goose becomes a veritable gas bomb. As the egg hit the target, it would explode with the noise of a firecracker, spraying the target with green, evil-smelling fluid. While enjoying this little game, I did not realize that the scheming mind of my sister was conjuring up something that was to be at my expense.

She was taking care of the goose eggs, while I handled the chicken eggs. Thinking that the goose egg, by its very size, would have a stronger shell than a hen's egg, she placed herself directly behind me. As I made the motion to throw it, extending my arm backward, she slightly tapped the egg I was getting ready to throw with the goose egg she was holding--thinking, of course, that she would break only the egg in my hand, leaving me with the green perfume all over me. But her calculation had not been quite correct, for it was a double explosion, spraying both of us. We dropped everything, running for home and gagging all the way.

When mother met us at the door, the minute she got the scent, she glared at us and shot her index finger out in the direction of the barn. Not able to sympathize with our plight, she had no intention of letting us use the bathtub. We had to be satisfied with the rain barrel that the hired hands used. All she did was bring us some clean clothing; the rain barrel had to do the rest. That was one practical joke that backfired on sister.

The Russian peasants all had large flocks of geese. They would come toddling over toward the mill like a company of drunken soldiers. There was always some spilled grain to be found. One flock arrived just as I was practicing handling a whip. I was wondering whether I could wrap the whip around one of those wobbling necks-- no harm in trying. To my surprise, the tongue of the whip had a sharper bite than I had anticipated. It struck a gosling and broke its neck. I watched the poor thing trying to raise its head. It just squatted there, flopping the limp head from side to side. I felt sorry. I did not have much time to mourn, however, for somewhere behind me there was a commotion. Two angry peasant women, each brandishing a stick, came running towards me. Since my instinct was much stronger than my reasoning powers, I dashed towards the mill. The babushkas did not dare to follow me there. They knocked at father's office door to register their complaint. Father, being a regular Solomon in solving problems of this kind, assured them that if they could catch me, they had his permission to administer justice to me in their own way. In the meantime, inside the mill I was safe.

Grandfather and Uncle John were always amused at my antics. Grandfather had a wide nose with an indentation in the center, giving it the appearance of two noses pressed together. I preferred to refer to it as grandfather's double nose. The remark would always turn his face crimson with laughter as he would jerk his chin up as if he were trying to pull his fat neck out of his shirt collar. For him I could do no wrong. Father often offered me fifty kopecks if I could sit for three minutes perfectly still. I was never able to collect.

However there were moments when my energy was directed in more useful and constructive channels. Watching the peasants mix cow dung with clay and use "mortar" to coat their adobe huts, I got the idea that a stucco cover of that type would look good on father's granary. The granary was built of heavy timber and boards, and an enterprising boy with artistic taste could do a lot to improve the front view at least. So one Sunday, when both father and mother were gone, I set to work. There was plenty of cow manure to be had, and the clay was no problem. First I carefully sealed the joints to make the surface smooth and even; over it came the coat of manure and loam plaster. Needless to say, the animal contribution made the plaster go on quite smoothly. Viewing my art, I was pleased and anxiously waited for my parents to come home. Looking toward the bridge, I saw the troika appearing. Proudly I waited. Father shook his head, but from that distance I could not tell whether it was out of admiration or disgust. I soon found out.

  He waved for me to come into the house. There was something different in the way he went about embracing me. I found myself stretched facedown over his knees. It dawned upon me that he did not appreciate my masterpiece as he went about impressing that fact upon me. He made me take a brush and soap and scrub every bit off. I learned that sometimes it is much harder to correct a mistake than to make one.

There suddenly appeared an intruder who would take a lot of fun out of our lives.

Father came home one day with a well-dressed gentleman.. The insignia over the visor of the stranger's cap indicated that he was a teacher. After father had introduced him to the family, he made the announcement that this gentleman would be our tutor and hold classes at our home every other day. If either of us was thrilled over the prospect of having to be entertained with books, we managed to hide it.

The teacher was a Bulgarian and by physical appearance seemed quite capable of handling a couple of youngsters. To begin the education process, he first laid down certain rules that we would have to observe. Coming unprepared to class meant staying after school to make up the neglected lesson. Misbehaving in class meant kneeling for about fifteen minutes, and disobeying meant a couple of well-placed strokes with a ruler over the open palm of one's hand.

Surprisingly, we both showed progress, and father and mother were proud.

After a while, we even got to like our teacher. We confided in him with many questions, and he always took great pains to explain things to us.

We had never seen a mirage before. When for the first time we saw this phenomenon in the sky--windmills turning, people moving about performing various tasks--it was as if we were observing life on some planet far away from the earth. Our teacher explained to us that what we were seeing were actual scenes taking place on earth, possibly many miles away. They were merely reflections, the moisture in the air acting as a mirror.

There were also tragic things happening. Not all people were as carefree and happy as we were.

Not far from the mill was a monastery. Every day one could see monks, two at a time, walking past the mill. One of these monks always walked alone. The rumor was that he was doing penance for his sins and had become mentally affected. One day, while the millhands were watching him, he stopped in front of the mill and started to ram his walking stick down his throat. The men rushed out to stop him. They rushed him to the hospital with blood all over him. The damage he had done to himself was grave enough to cause his death. He kept insisting to the very end that it was God's will that he should punish himself for his own sins and that only then would he receive absolution and peace for his soul. To me, who loved life so much, it was inconceivable that anyone could be so foolish as to take his life.

To my sister and me, life was just one happy day following another. The only thing that saddened me very much was to see father get one of his asthma attacks. They were becoming more frequent. He was allergic to mill dust, and the doctors called it "miller's asthma." Some nights when I could not hear him breathe, I would start to cry. Then I would hear his voice from across the room: "*Bueble*, [little boy] why are you crying?" Sobbing, I would answer that since I could not hear him breathe I was afraid he had died. He then would assure me that he felt fine and would tell me to go back to sleep. What a wonderful feeling it was to have that assurance! To me he was the greatest man on earth. Even though he was a busy man, one could barge right into his office and ask him questions, and he was never too busy to give an answer.

When he was worried, he had the habit of walking up and down the floor. Coming alongside of him, I would put my arm around one of his strong legs and keep step with him. He would offer me his open palm as a chin rest. So father and son walked the floor together, helping each other with their problems.

To get relief for the asthmatic condition, he began to take trips to various health resorts. One was at Pyatigorsk, near the Black Sea, and the other was Bad Nauheim, in Germany. They always seemed to help him, but the attacks always returned as soon as he entered the mill again. The local doctors prescribed a certain cigar made out of some native weed--it would loosen his cough, but outside of that, it was just so much quackery. To get away from the mill was the only alternative.

We always looked forward to the times when John came home for his vacation. He was rooming in Krasnodar with an Armenian family and in the course of time had acquired the ability to understand that language. I admired him in his gray uniform. It gave me great pleasure to put on his blue and white striped cap and strut around the room. To keep me from ruining his cap, he produced a metal anchor and had mother sew it on my cap just above the visor. As he put it, "Now you are an admiral in the navy." I was satisfied. It gave me prestige, and I left his cap alone.

John was a real bookworm and always followed some hobby that improved his knowledge. His skill in catching butterflies with a net was fascinating to me. He had a number of cigar boxes with glass lids on them. In these boxes he put some green wine leaves that served the various caterpillars as they spun their cocoons around themselves and later emerged as beautiful butterflies. He explained the process of metamorphosis to us, and we looked upon him as some sort of scientist.

Aside from his hobbies, he was a *balalaika* and guitar player. The songs he sang were, as a rule, of a revolutionary nature. I soon learned some of the lyrics and would sing along with him. He stressed, however, the fact that I should never sing these songs away from home; otherwise, the Czar would have me sent to Siberia. John was always more Russian than German.

At one time when he, father, and Uncle John were discussing politics at the dinner table, he got so angry that he picked up a fork and threw it at the Czar's picture hanging on the wall. The fork stuck right in the Czar's forehead. Of course, father would deliberately offer opinions that would get my brother excited. It upset him just to hear his father downgrading socialism.

Something that caused a lot of glee was hearing mother carrying on a conversation in Russian. Whenever there was a knock at the door, we were all pretty sure that the visitor was a Russian. Mother, answering the door, would pleadingly look back over her shoulder, expecting someone to come to her assistance, since her Russian vocabulary was limited; but no one would make a move. Everyone kept silent in order to hear the conversation. For mother it was always two parts German and one part Russian. As soon as she had gotten rid of the visitor, she pretended to be looking for a stick or strap with which to clear the room. Everybody ran for the door, laughing and mimicking her Russian accent and vocabulary. Mom was a good sport, though. Even father enjoyed teasing her. She was also the religious member of the family. I cannot remember ever having seen father in church. Mother, on the other hand, would not miss a prayer meeting if at all possible. She would even on occasion visit a Russian Baptist meeting. She was a prolific reader and well informed in all kinds of literature. She also had such beautiful handwriting that some people doubted the letters had been handwritten. She was just as familiar with Greek mythology and German sagas as she was with the Bible stories. Sister and I would be spellbound, listening to her telling some of those stories.

Despite father's lack of interest in the church, there was no one more respected than he. His great sense of humor and warmth created for him a regular "fan club." Some would hang around just for laughs. But even though father was the definite head of the family, we had to give mother credit for being the neck that controlled the head. In her quiet way, she knew exactly how to cool father down whenever his temper caused him to fly into a rage. Quietly, not saying a word in defense, she would keep busy doing something while at the same time sniffing and "turning on the sprinklers." The minute he saw tears, it was all over, for the lion became a lamb, and it was heartwarming to hear him purring and apologizing.

Mother was also a great lover of pets. She could never be without them. In addition to dogs, cats, and birds, she had a horse as a pet. She had bottle-fed a white-faced chestnut colt that had lost its mother, and had raised it. Whenever Mittya saw mother anywhere in the yard and was either watering or unhitching the horses, he always managed to turn Masha, the chestnut mare, loose to see what she would do. Masha immediately would trot over to mother and nuzzle her either for a handout or affection. Mother would put her arms around Masha's neck and talk to her as she would have to one of her children. This touching relationship ended in bitter tears.

Mittya had to take father to Stavropol on one of his usual business trips. Since father would be gone for several days, the hired hand always returned home until it was time to return and pick up father again.

We saw the coach approaching, but the white blaze of Masha was not in evidence. There were only two horses. The chestnut mare was missing. Mother was immediately apprehensive. She ran towards the coach, shouting, "Where is Masha?"

Mittya, thinking he would break the news gently, did exactly the wrong thing. Without answering, he turned, reached back, and pulled off a tarpaulin, revealing the hide of mother's beloved pet. Mother stared at it for a moment, then gave the most painful-sounding cry as she ran back into the house, weeping. It was as if one of her children had died. After she had composed herself, she came back out and gave the stableboy strict orders to bury the hide and not to think of having it tanned.

To compound mother's grief, something else happened the same week. She had a Pekinese puppy that followed me to the home of one of the neighbors.

The Russians always had some vicious dogs around. A big *buika* (wolfhound) came darting out and made for the little Pekinese. Before

I could ward him off, he had the little puppy in his mouth, shaking it as if it were a rat, then laid it down. I ran over to pick it up; there was blood oozing out of both flanks. It kept gasping for breath. The beast had bitten clear through the tiny body. I started to cry, cradling the mortally wounded pet in my arms as I ran for home.

Mother tried to administer first aid, but there was no saving it. Gasping a few more times, it died. It seems that misfortunes always have relatives following.

But there were also moments of joy and laughter. For instance, watching the Russian women on a hot summer day at the community well as they were getting water for household use was interesting. Since the water from an ordinary well was unusable for human consumption, the *stanitza* had community wells in different sections of the village. One of the wells was directly in front of the mill. The women were mostly teenage girls carrying water with a wooden shoulder yoke, a pail dangling from either side.

While they congregated around the well, usually in the later afternoon, we knew that sooner or later something would happen, and we always waited for it. One of the maidens would accidentally spill some cold water on someone. That would be the signal for everyone to get into the action. They would drench one another with cold water, chasing one another around the well. During that playtime, any passerby had to give wide berth if he did not want to wind up soaked from head to foot. The Russian girls did not wear brassieres or any kind of support, and it was quite a sight to see these buxom lasses running, screaming, and laughing.

Then suddenly one of them would start a song; and before she had finished the first sentence, the entire group would fall into a mighty chorus. These choruses could be heard from other groups in all directions. One wonders why it is that oppressed people always resort to singing and dancing. It was the Russian peasants' specialty. Invariably, the first song was:

"The sun rises and the sun sets,
    But in prison it's always dark.
Day after day the sentry
    Guards my window.
Guard and watch however you like,
    I am not going to escape.
No desire for freedom
    And these chains I cannot break."

It was a song of the peasants' submissiveness.

    They walked around, their feet wrapped in *lapty* (burlap) held together with twine, and yet they had reasons to sing. The Russian peasant was all heart. Returning from their watermelon patches, they could not pass the mill without stopping to leave a few melons at our house.

Some of the peasants bringing wheat to the mill also brought sunflower seeds or mustard seeds to be pressed into oil. It was fascinating to watch the process. The seeds were first slightly roasted; then equal amounts were wrapped in square pieces of cloth and put into vertical tubes about twelve inches in diameter. Upon every deposit was put a metal disk with many holes in it. The process was repeated until the tubes were filled. Then came the plunger that was applied ever tighter to start the oil flowing. The peasants, who always had their wooden bowls handy, lost no time in filling them and sampling the oil. Dunking their black bread into a bowl of sunflower seed oil was a real feast for them.

The pressing done, the husks had

turned into solid disks like huge poker chips. It made splendid cattle fodder and was sold to the rich land barons in the vicinity.

Occasionally father went on a tour of inspection to make sure the peasants had not brought any vodka on the premises. There was to be absolutely no drinking in and around the mill. Some of the huge belts keeping the wheels turning were capable of tearing off a person's arm. If father spied a bottle anywhere, it always ended up smashed against a *trosha* wheel. No one ever challenged his authority. It was rather ironic that a man who had such stern ways about him could be so admired and liked by employees as well as customers.

One of the peasants' favorite sports was to goad father into displaying his physical strength. They would always start by teasing him: "Gottlieb Bogdanowitch, we all agree that under your fancy coat there is nothing but fat and no muscles. We are convinced that you could not even lift a sack of wheat from the *droshka*." Of course, father, knowing what they were after, was always willing to oblige and humor them. Walking over to their wagons, he would grab a sack with each hand and pull two of them down at the same time. Like children, they would clap their hands and laugh. The peasant was always a child.

On Sundays when the mill was not operating, the peasants would nevertheless congregate in front of the mill to hear father reading the newspaper to them. The Russo-Japanese war was in progress and they were concerned about their sons who were at the front. This practice got my father into severe trouble later on.

The mutiny of the sailors on the *Potyomking*, a cruiser anchored in the Odessa harbor, was the signal for a general uprising all over Russia. The government went immediately into action to round up and prosecute the dissidents. Cossacks were dispatched to all trouble areas to make arrests. A company of these trouble shooters appeared in our *stanitza*. They bivouacked near the mill, requisitioning our well for watering and bathing their horses. The officer commanding the cossacks was a very amiable man and often visited our home. Mother always had some eggs and butter for him, for which he was very grateful.

One day the officer came to us with some very distressing news. He had brought with him a list of names of those that were to be arrested, and my father headed the list. After my father explained to him that his only crime was that he had been reading the newspaper to the peasants, the officer was sympathetic and advised father to contact the local authorities in order to get his name removed from the list. After many trips and a good deal of bribing, father managed to have his name removed.

Many of the others listed ended their lives on the gallows.

Despite this near-tragic event, grandfather and Uncle John had something with which they could tease father. But the noose had been too close for comfort.

When brother came home that summer, he told us what had happened in Krasnodar. He had taken part in a student protest march, singing revolutionary songs. The girls taking part in the march, at a given signal, all raised their dresses, displaying embroidered in red on their petticoats, the words: *"Zar daloy!"* ("Down with the Czar.") A company of cossacks rode down on them and hit the students on their heads with their *nahaikas* (riding whips which had little lead balls at the ends). They soon had the marchers running for cover. Needless to say, the scare had quite a calming effect on the revolutionaries in our family. Through the ordeal the district attorney (Prisyaschny Poverny) and father had become friends, and the attorney quite often visited our home.

Every once in a while either my sister or I would be permitted to come along with father on his trips to Stavropol. It was always a great thrill. We had heard that the Caucasus Robin Hood (Salim Khan) was active in the nearby mountains. My mind would conjure up all kinds of possibilities. I imagined an outlaw behind every bush or tree. Besides, why should father always be traveling with a loaded revolver in his traveling bag and have a rifle lying on the floor of the coach? We always referred to the revolver as the American gun. It was a Colt. But in that respect, the only time a gun was fired was when some wolves were showing too much interest and came too close. A shot in their direction would always scatter them in a hurry.

Sometimes the horses would suddenly raise their heads, prick their ears, and snort, indicating that they were afraid. It was always an indication that there were camels approaching from somewhere. As a rule, it did not take long before one could hear the whining of the ill-tempered beasts. Mittya always had trouble controlling the team at such times, and often the *troika* would leave the road and take the coach for a distance over rough ground, and the coachman would not be able to get back onto the road until the caravan had passed.

There was one trip that we will never forget. It was in mid-winter, and mother decided to visit a friend in a neighboring village. She took sister and me along. While on the way, we suddenly found ourselves in a snowstorm. Visibility had gotten so bad that we could hardly see the horses ahead of us. We were getting panicky and could hear mother quietly praying. Mittya confessed that we were no more on the road and that we were lost, not knowing in which direction we were headed. The terrain in that area was quite dangerous; so he suggested that we let the horses have free rein. They would at least keep us from going over some embankment. After some time we came upon a Russian mud hut and inquired as to our whereabouts. The peasant told us that we were not too far from the mill and invited us to stay until visibility had returned. The team of horses had made almost a complete circle around the *stanitza* but brought us home safely.

When father returned home and found out about our experience, he naturally reprimanded mother for having taken such a risk, especially since she was expecting a baby in the near future. Well, it was something we were not likely to repeat.

The happy moment came when our beautiful baby sister Rosalia came into our lives. The day she was born the maid brought the baby into our room to show it off. Sister Maria was hysterical with joy; but I, on the other hand, was sulking. I was jealous. To me the baby was an intruder and took all the attention away from me. I did not even want to look at it and told the maid to take it away.

My jealousy did not last long. Soon I was at the head of all the admirers and became very fond of her. She had big black eyes and cute dimples in her cheeks when she smiled. Whenever mother was nursing her, I would kneel close by, watching. I would reach over and pull the nipple out of baby's mouth, and as if she knew that I was playing a game, she would look at me and smile. After she went back to nursing again, I pretended to repeat the same thing. This time, however, mother took Rosalia's hand and the minute I was about to pull the nipple again, slapped my hand with the baby's hand. That would make her laugh so hard

that she often got the hiccoughs.
She knew that I was playing a game with her, and after a while whenever mother got ready, the baby kept looking for me. It was hard to tell what she enjoyed more, the nursing or the game.

Rosalia grew rapidly into a beautiful child. The doctor who came to our home always said that he would not get married but wait for Rosalia to grow up. She would be his bride. This happy child, born into this euphoric family, was later in life to experience the greatest pain and agony that the Soviet-made hell could devise. But of this I shall write later.

The millhands all had a hand in spoiling the boss's son. The firemen let him help stoke the boilers and crawl along inside the boilers to chisel away the slag.

The miller showed me how to test the flour and tell whether the rollers were too tight, in which event the flour had a scorched scent. To play a practical joke on father, I would run into his office with a handful of flour, telling him that the flour smelled scorched. He would ask me to let him smell it, whereupon I brought it up to his nose so quickly that most of the flour was left in his beard. I ran out laughing.

The only place strictly forbidden to me was the machine room, unless someone was with me. The machinist, Metro, who was also the father of Mittya, made up for it by letting me come into the blacksmith shop. Here I had a free hand and could do my blacksmithing or carpenter work to my heart's content.

He made me a toy that was called a buzzer. If one tied it on a string and swung it around the head in a circular motion similar to a lariat, it made the sound of a swarm of bees. I kept walking around the yard making this noise until I came close to the pigpen. The pigs did not like the noise at all and got very excited. They ran back and forth making funny grunting noises. It occurred to me that I should step inside the pen to show them that there was nothing to be afraid of. I made the mistake of leaving the gate open.

I had barely started to swing the buzzer when all the pigs bolted past me out the gate and into the open. Luckily Mittya and one of the other hands had seen what happened. They immediately mounted and rode after the snorting herd and brought them back again. That particular adventure brought me aftereffects that I was not soon to forget, especially when sitting down. This time it was not father but mother who, armed with a flexible willow stick, put her point across quite effectively. The pigs were rid of their tormenter for good.

An annual event that everybody looked forward to was the

fish-and-shrimp fry held every year. Early in the summer father took all his employees out to a certain river for a picnic. Two men would drag a net for fish and shrimp. One man would wade in until the water reached his armpits; the other one was closer to the shore. Every so often they would drag the net to the shore, and the bouncing catch would be gathered into a large tub, the shrimp into a different container. I had no sympathy for the fish, for they were dead when they reached the frying pans, but I felt bad about the shrimp. They were cast alive into a kettle of boiling water. Of course, they were soon past pain, but it seemed cruel to me. Once the shrimp had put on their festive red coats, everything was forgotten--for I enjoyed eating shrimp more than anything else. Unfortunately, these happy events were soon to be permanently interrupted.

## Chapter 4
## A TRAGIC EVENT BRINGS SORROW

FATHER WAS AWAY TO SPEND some time at the Pyatigorsk health resort seeking relief from his asthma. We were awakened at midnight one night by a commotion outside. All our windows were covered with shutters, so that we had no way of looking out. What suddenly struck terror to our hearts was the cry of "*Bozcscar!*" ("Fire!") Mother ran and jerked the door open. It was as light outside as midday. The mill was one huge inferno. The heat was so intense that it was almost impossible to stand in the open doorway. Long orange tongues were licking the sky. The fire-fighting equipment was utterly useless. Despite the super-human effort at the pumps, the stream of water did not do any good. The

crackling and noises that we heard
as the heavy machinery dropped
through the upper floor was terrible.
We just had to stand by and watch
our mill burn to the ground until
there was nothing but crumbling
walls looking like ancient ruins.
We stood close to mother holding
on to her; she was sobbing loudly.
People were running to and fro in
utter confusion, panic-stricken.

For three days there were smoldering ashes and smoke rising, filling
the air with the obnoxious odor that
ever reminded us of our shattered
dreams. People living twenty miles
away and seeing the glow on the
horizon remarked, "A blaze like that
could only be caused by the Kalmbach
mill."

The thought that was uppermost in
the minds of all was, How would
father take it? We had no way of
contacting him, and he was not due

home until several days later. We kept looking down toward the wooden bridge, anxiously waiting for the familiar sight. Finally the *troika* appeared. It was now coming at full speed. Coming to an abrupt stop in the middle of the yard, father sat perfectly still for what seemed a very long time. He had his back turned toward us, and the heavy fur collar obscured his entire head. Then he slowly rose and stepped down. He walked toward his family. Gone was that familiar proud stride. The man coming toward us was bent under a crushing burden. He looked like a beaten man. We waited for him to speak. The first word that came from his mouth was, "Besmenoff." That was the name of our chief competitor across the river. Besmenoff had been in business only a short while. He had grandiose ideas and had erected a flour mill powered by burning oil. But for some reason he seemed unable to get into full swing. At the same time he could not help but see his competitor's mill puffing steam all day long. On several occasions attempts had been made to sabotage our mill, but there was never any definite proof that Besmenoff had been behind them despite father's conviction.

This time the arsonist had waited until he knew that father would be gone for some time. Investigation uncovered the fact that the fire had definitely been started in the oil mill. The arsonist had made sure that the fire would spread fast, for once the oil mill was ablaze there would be nothing to stop the fire from spreading to the adjoining building.

The watchman on duty was either asleep or bribed. But the misfortune did not keep father down too long. He tried to cheer up his family by saying, "If Besmenoff thinks he has me beaten, he had better guess again!"

On the following day he called all his employees together and made known his decision to rebuild the mill. The employees were hysterical and cheered. They were all willing to become just common laborers and start clearing away the debris. Soon caravans of loaded wagons started to arrive from different directions, bringing bricks, mortar, and lumber. The bricklayers and assemblymen followed. It was obvious that the new structure would dwarf the old one and there would be no comparison. Modern machinery arrived from Germany and Austria. If Besmenoff thought that the mill he had burned had been too much competition, he now had real cause to worry.

The mill was built. The giant smokestack, belching smoke all day long, was a daily reminder to the evil man across the river that it had been his own doing that had produced this present menace.

The peasants also spread the rumor that Besmenoff was supposed to have been the culprit in causing the fire and showed their sympathy in patronizing our mill instead of his.

Though business was again in full swing, everything was not the same anymore. We all noticed that a change had come over father. He was extremely restless and walked the floor more than ever. When I walked beside him in the usual manner, he would as usual cup his hand under my chin. But it did not feel the same; the warmth and reassurance did not come through. His worry obviously was more serious than ever before. Then it happened.

A heart attack! On top of his asthma, now a weakened heart. The doctor's prognosis was that unless he left the mill entirely he would not live much longer. He was to have complete rest. Grandfather and Uncle John persuaded him to leave; they would carry on. Father, however, did hire a general manager who was experienced in running a mill. He was a Volga German by the name of David Kindsfatter. Grandfather was getting too old, and Uncle John was still single.

    We moved away to the nearest German village.

## Chapter 5
## THE GERMAN VILLAGE OF BLUMENFELD

BLUMENFELD WAS ONLY ABOUT fifteen miles from the mill; so it was not too difficult to keep in touch. Uncle John served as messenger, bringing the reports and keeping father informed.

Almost adjoining the village was the larger village of Friederichsfeld. Both villages were predominantly Baptist, which made mother feel very happy. Here she could attend her beloved prayer meetings to her heart's content. Neither of these villages could be compared to our village of Dolinowka. Instead of ornate brick walls along the front yards facing the street, there were just mud fences. These people came from the Odessa district and spoke a dialect quite unfamiliar to us and called themselves Kersonians, the name referring to the district from which they had come, Kerson.

For sister and me this was a new adventure. Here we were to have a lot of friends. The property we acquired had been owned by a tavern-keeper. The tavern facing the street was boarded shut. Apparently the Baptists did not patronize it sufficiently. The entire property seemed out of place and did in no way conform with the architecture of the other homes. It had a hip roof covered with sheet metal and painted blue. Mother was very much pleased with the interior of the home. It had shiny oak floors; and instead of the usual three rooms, it had five spacious rooms. It was the only solid brick structure in the neighborhood. Behind the house there was an enclosed small fruit orchard and flower garden. In the middle of the garden was a bath cabin. The bathhouse apparently had not seen much service and had been used as a toolshed. When my brother John came home to spend his summer vacation, he fixed it all up so it was in operating condition. The water tank overhead had to be filled manually, but it still was an improvement over a rain barrel. The spray was released by means of a chain.

Not very far behind the property there was a valley running parallel to the village. It was just right for winter sports. Those children who did not own a sled would scoot down on a "flying saucer" borrowed from their mother's kitchen. Any piece of metal big enough to sit on would take one down the hill.

For those who were older and preferred skating, there was always the frozen stream at the bottom of the hill.

Farther down in the valley one could see the Kalmuck camp. It resembled an Indian camp, but the tents had the shape of huge cakes with slightly sloped tops. They were made out of animal skins with heavy matting reinforcing the walls inside to insure proper warmth. We often wandered down and played with the children in the camp. The Kalmucks were the village herdsmen.

Every morning one of the first sounds one heard was the sound of a ram's horn. It was the signal for the villagers to get their stock ready and turn it out on the street. The horses were gathered first, followed by the cows; then came the sheep, and then the calves not yet accustomed to herd life.

With the calves the herdsmen had to have the help of the village children at least for a few mornings until they could be properly handled. The children always looked forward to this happy event. It was a joy to see some of the young calves with their tails in the air, trying to bolt away from the herd, with laughing and screaming youngsters chasing after them to get them back into the group.

All the herdsmen carried special selected hickory or oak clubs. Each club had a cluster of metal rings fastened to its end so that it was balanced for throwing. In most cases, it would only have to be shaken; the sound of the metal rings would convey the message to stragglers to return to the herd. Ignoring that warning sound would mean that the well-directed club would come flying in their direction --with painful consequences.

Once in a while a Kalmuck would return with his herd in the evening with the carcass of a dead wolf draped over his pony behind the saddle. The herdsmen carried no guns but on their swift Mongolian ponies would chase the predators until they were exhausted, then ride alongside. A well-directed blow on the head would end the chase, and the wolf, with a crushed skull, would soon have his pelt warming a grateful herdsman.

The Kalmucks were a friendly and hospitable people. If one wandered into their camp, they always invited one to share their food with them. The food was not too appetizing (they were known to pick up dead chicken by the roadside, shake off the maggots, and take it home to cook it).

The news that Uncle John brought from time to time was not good. Grandfather, due to his advanced age, begged to be relieved of his duty so he and grandmother could enjoy a few years in retirement. With grandfather gone, that left Uncle John alone with the general manager.

To rebuild the mill, father obviously had to go heavily into debt. His not being able to look after his business himself worried his creditors. The banks demanded payment and threatened to foreclose.

To compound the dilemma, father, on top of asthma and a weak heart, suffered a slight stroke, leaving the right side of his face paralyzed. Although he overcame the paralysis, the pressure had become too great for him. He had to let the creditors have their way. They pounced on him like wolves.

Uncle John had for some time contemplated marriage, and now the proper time had come. He married a girl from the village of Friederichsfeld and accepted an agency selling Singer sewing machines. This life, however, was not to his liking, and he soon gave it up by following in grandfather's footsteps to become a schoolteacher.

To father it had become increasingly clear that he would not have much longer to live; so he decided to move the family back to our home village of Dolinowka. There we would again be among our own people and could depend on grandfather Belz to help us if need be.

## Chapter 6
### BACK TO DOLINOWKA

WE RETURNED TO OUR HOME village practically broke. It was a humiliation for all of us. Grandfather Belz was sympathetic and let us move into one of his houses that we at one time owned. He also had jobs for everyone in the family except father and baby sister Rosalia. Father was too sick and sister was too young.

Maria joined the staff of housemaids, making them four altogether, and mother was entrusted with the job of field overseer. It was her job to keep a group of Russian girls, hired to hoe the sunflower fields, busy. I, too, had to keep up my end and work right alongside them. As always, I had to turn the work into a game and always challenged my neighbor to a race to the end of the field. This spurt of energy soon would have us way ahead of the rest of them--until the "boss lady" came to inspect our work. She would call my attention to the fact that some of the weeds in my row had been merely knocked dizzy and the rest buried. It meant for me to go back and do the work over again--to the delight of the other field-hands, who enjoyed laughing and teasing me. But it all made the work fun.

Father's illness had become critical. Often he would lapse into delirium, uttering incoherent sentences, speaking of experiences that he must have had while traveling around. It was the first time we had ever heard the word *banana* mentioned. Brother John explained to us that it was a fruit he had acquired a taste for when he was abroad. Despite his severe suffering, he still showed concern for his family. It hurt him to see his family destitute and at the mercy of other people. He was such a proud man. Sometimes he would reach out and take my hand, looking at the blisters inside my palms, then silently press me to his heart.

He was a pathetic figure. His legs had swollen to twice their size and it was difficult for him to move about the house. Mother had an instrument that worked somewhat like a staple gun. When applied to his legs, it would release a spring, puncturing his skin with many sharp needle points. An ugly-looking liquid, mixed with blood, would run down his legs--it was done obviously to relieve the dropsical condition in his legs.

One morning, as we were sitting at the breakfast table, father came shuffling into the room with a radiant smile on his face. We all looked up at him, apprehensive, thinking that perhaps his mind had become affected. Standing close to the table, he said: "Children, this morning you are looking at a new father. Last night I accepted Jesus into my heart. I have never experienced greater happiness in my entire life. Now I am not afraid to die, and I want all of you to rejoice with me. Do not pray for me anymore to get well. God will soon be coming for me to take me to the heavenly home, where we will all see each other again."

His entire face was aglow with happiness. Of course, the only one who appreciated what he had said was mother. She got up and embraced him, tears of joy trickling down her cheeks. But the boy who worshiped him merely raised the cup to his face in order to hide the tears that came to him. Silently he wept into his cup and, to quote the poet Lermontov, "was drinking the bitter cup of life with tears moistening the rim of his cup." Again I felt that big soft hand on my head as I heard father say, "My *bueble* always has tears." He continued, "Soon I will be gone, but I know that God will take care of you." There was only one choice left, and that was to get him to a hospital in Krasnodar as quickly as possible. John was in his last year in school and could look in on him and keep the family informed. The hospitalization did not last too long.

One night mother was very restless and could not sleep. She told us that she kept hearing father calling for her and that she must hurry to his bedside. She went to grandfather that very night and told him what had happened. He was very understanding and let her have a team and driver. She was gone only an hour or two; then we heard a knock at the door. It was brother John, who had come to report father's death. He also told us that as they passed a vehicle coming in the opposite direction, the voice of mother reached him through the pitch-dark night: "John, is that you?" And when he answered, she continued, "Father has died."

Mother often surprised us with her intuition. As it happened, father had died that very same night and according to the attending nurse kept calling mother's name, pleading for her to come to him.

It took several days for the coffin bringing father's body for burial to arrive. Embalming was not the custom; and due to the midsummer heat, when the body did arrive an offensive odor was already noticeable. Knowing that this was our beloved father lying there subject to the inevitable laws of nature was traumatic.

The time for burial had come. Six strong pallbearers carried him out to the cemetery while the church bells kept tolling. The family was following on foot directly behind the coffin. The odor was almost unbearable. The little twelve-year-old boy could only think and feel that soft hand under his chin as he used to walk up and down the room beside his father. That boy felt as if his entire chest was occupied by a swelling heart that was to explode any moment. Big teardrops rolled down his cheeks. He kept thinking, Why did God take my father away. He was only forty-six years old.

Arriving at the open grave, the coffin was brought to rest on some beams laid across the gaping hole. The schoolmaster read the burial ritual, and the casket was lowered into the grave. The family and friends started weeping loudly. Heavy clumps of dirt began to hit the wooden coffin, filling the vicinity with dust. The pallbearers kept shoveling in dirt until there was an oval pile covering the grave. What a horrible memory for a sensitive boy to carry away with him! My happy childhood was buried with him; I had experienced a change within me, and henceforth my life would be different.

The first year following father's death was the hardest. Readjustment did not come easy. Grandfather took care of us, but we had the feeling that is was more out of a sense of tradition than out of compassion. He treated us like servants. Our poor mother was often seen silently wiping her eyes as she watched her children work alongside other hired hands. To think that just a short time ago she was giving orders to her servants and now had to be a servant herself.

But as the German philosopher so aptly stated, "The fleetest beast to bear one to perfection is suffering." Even though father's demise was a painful experience for the family, he left us a legacy beyond evaluation--the memory that he had been a good father.

Grandfather and I did not get along well at all. Subconsciously I resented the fact that he was taking father's place and giving me orders. The only time he ever had a kind word for me was when he received some correspondence in Russian from his tenants in the Tashkent area. Then he called on me to read the letters to him, since he himself was unable to read them. Yes, he was the richest man in the village but by no means the most liked. It was no wonder that one of his underlings was heard to say, "If revolution ever comes, he will have to be taken care of first."

We had to take our meals with the servants in the basement. Mother was the only one permitted complete freedom of the house and also the only one permitted to sit at the grandparents' table.

The old man in his shepherd years had sustained a severe spine injury which had left him deformed; he walked with the right hand extending below his knee. It was always my own contention that grandfather had gotten that way from picking up rusty nails.

Once I managed to get up into the attic. Poking around, I found his old shepherd's crook and a pair of leather pants, relics of his earlier days.

Grandmother, despite her advanced age, was a beautiful woman. Her back was as straight as a ramrod. She spent her days in the flower garden or tending to her bees. Getting a suntan was not the fashion, but just the opposite. She always wore a wide-brimmed hat and had her arms well protected from the sun's rays with removable sleeves. Some of the younger men would often tease her maids by saying, "Grandmother is the prettiest one in the bunch." It was evident that grandmother enjoyed her wealth, and her home was her castle.

With its shiny oak floors and mahogany woodwork, the house was stocked with period furniture; all the chairs had needlepoint covering. The massive oak canopy bed was a conversation piece. Whenever the minister made his periodic visits to the village, the Belz home was his headquarters. A life-size picture of the arrogant Kaiser Wilhelm hung on the wall, and the room had the appearance of a small museum.

The following account will clearly reveal how grandfather and I got along. The wind had done some damage to one of the haystacks. All the servants were out in the field; so it was up to grandfather and me to make the repairs. He had me crawl up on the haystack on a ladder and kept giving me instructions on how to adjust the cables and logs that kept the hay from blowing away. He was beginning to irritate me. I gave one of the logs a temperamental shove, and it rolled down the side of the stack and happened to strike him on the head, knocking him down. Grandfather did not believe that it was an accident and had me come down. By the time I reached the ground, he had armed himself with a sturdy grapevine, which he laid across my back several times. He went to mother to register his complaint, saying, "Paul almost kills one, and all he can say is "Oh-oh!". Naturally, when I came home that evening, mother asked me for my version of the incident. When I removed my shirt to show her the welts across my back, she sadly shook her head and said, "Son, we will soon leave here for good."

Brother John by this time had graduated from the *Gimnasium* (college) and had found employment with the Volga Commercial

Bank of Krasnodar. He wrote and informed us that he would now be able to take care of us, and asked us to get ready to move to the city. But again an unfortunate accident caused us to postpone our departure.

Grandfather had just given me an order to fill a canteen with drinking water as we were getting ready for a field trip. As I handed him the canteen, I almost fell against the wagon and had to hold on. He noticed that something was wrong and touched my forehead--I was burning up with fever. This time he knew that I was not faking and sent me home. Mother, who was quite knowledgeable in recognizing symptoms, immediately concluded that I had typhus and put me to bed. By the following morning my little sister had also come down with it. We were two very sick children. For some time the only food permitted was liquid--even the water had to be boiled.

Every time the church bells would toll, signifying that someone had died, it was generally the guess of the villagers that it was one of the Kalmbach children. But mother was a competent nurse and pulled us through. Rosalia was on the opposite side of the room, so that mother kept walking back and forth across the room to keep cold compresses on our foreheads. The spells of delirium were frightening; the sensation that walls were closing in on one defies description. After we were out of danger, there was the problem of keeping solid food away for some time, because it was still dangerous to consume anything but liquids. We were ravenously hungry.

One day when mother was gone, hunger drove me to break into the locked bread box to get something to eat. When mother came home and learned what happened, she remarked, "Son, it's a wonder that you are still alive." She again explained how important it was for us to wait just a little while longer.

We both completely recovered and were soon ready for our move to Krasnodar to live with John. Becoming once more a self-supporting family gave one a pleasant feeling.

## Chapter 7
### EXCITING CITY LIFE

SISTER MARIA DECIDED TO STAY with the grandparents. She had a way with grandfather that was quite effective. She even dared to contradict him at times, and he seemed to enjoy it. The fact that the three other maids in his service were granddaughters from his former marriage helped to create harmony among them. Anyway, for Maria there was more of a future in the village. She eventually married one of his grandsons.

Brother John had rented a cottage from a storekeeper. The dwelling was in the backyard behind the store. To get to it we had to walk by a pile of coal, which made it imperative that mother always leave a rag in front of the door so we could wipe our feet before entering the house. None of us liked our new surroundings, and it was obvious that we would not stay there very long.

For mother there was always something to worry about. Barely had I gotten over the typhus when I contracted malaria. After the daily dose of quinine I would have to sit in a sunny spot until the chills left. Once the fever was gone, I lost no time in exploring the city. Sometimes in the evening, after John came home from the bank, he would ask me where I had been during the day. When I told him, he would laughingly shake his head and say, "I have been living in this city for eight years and never knew there were such places."

Looking for new living quarters had become my task. Every day I made my daily route looking for vacancies. The owners most of the time showed slight amusement at seeing such a young prospective renter but were always friendly and showed me through. If the house impressed me, I would arrange for brother and mother to see it.

Within a few blocks from the inns where most of the villagers stayed overnight whenever they brought their wheat to the market, I discovered the ideal place. From there I could always walk down to the inns and make my daily search by looking over the registers for people from the village. The house belonged to a cossack colonel.

The property was surrounded by a seven-foot fence. When I yanked the chain by the gate, I could hear a couple of angry dogs rushing to greet me. Soon I heard the stern command, "*Posholl won!*" "Be gone!" It was the voice of the cossack orderly, who came across the yard from the colonel's home to open the gate. When I told him that I was interested in the vacancy, he showed me through. The minute I stepped across the threshold

I knew that I had found our next home. The appointment was made for that very evening to have mother and brother see it.

Again, the orderly showed us through. Both of them liked the house. The cossack went to call his boss. Soon the colonel appeared, and with him his son, who was about my age. While the officer and brother came to an agreement, the son and I struck up a conversation. The colonel noticed it and smiled; he was obviously pleased.

The first month's rent was paid, and we went home and got ready to move.

Mother was particularly pleased by the fact that it was only a couple of blocks from the market, where she could do her daily grocery shopping. For a few days we had a problem with the dogs. We had to keep bribing them until they were convinced that we belonged.

I made my daily pilgrimage to the inns. Walking through the yards, I was always able to tell which vehicles belonged to the Germans. The inns had a brass band playing in the *trackteer* (restaurant), which made my visits quite exciting.

At home the officer's son and I had erected our cricket field; and often, after he came home from school, we would have a game.

Brother, in the meantime, was making an effort to end my idle days. He came home with the news that he had landed a job for me in the bank where he was employed. That way he could keep an eye on me, and at the same time I would be some help to the family. I was to be one of the two messenger boys that the bank employed. There were about thirty employees in the bank, and about half the desks had bells that we had to respond to. The other boy, Kolya, was a very friendly lad and had served in the bank for some time. With him to break me in, the adjustment was very easy. Since he, too, had a penchant for mischief, we got along well. Kolya had perfected a system whereby we were able to collect quite a few tips during the day. We had a list of bank customers who we knew could be depended on to give tips. All one of these customers had to do was to wink at one of us, and the process was set in motion. They were usually clients who were in a hurry to do their business and get out. Now, the documents which had to be carried from one bank official to the other for signature sometimes piled up on the desk. We worked on a first-come-first-served basis, and we would always put the latest paper to be signed on the bottom of the pile, except in the case of someone who winked at either of us. That meant that his document, whatever, would wind up on top of the pile, thus permitting him to leave the bank long

before the first comers. The rest
of the employees knew our tricks
and were amused, watching a pair of
"hustlers" at work.

The job completed, all depending
on who took care of the client, said
messenger boy would station himself in the exit hall in such a way
that the bribe could be received without anyone's seeing it. There were
two uniformed policemen stationed
in the hall, but they very conveniently
managed to have their backs turned.

It made me feel proud to come
home and drop a few extra coins in my
mother's lap. A certain amount was
always deposited in a piggy bank, add-
ing to a Christmas fund. I always
made sure that I had enough money
to buy each member of the family a
Christmas present. I will never
forget one particular Christmas.

I had purchased for mother a
lovely embroidered shawl; sister
Maria, a bottle of perfume; and

Rosalia, a mama doll. I gave my brother John a cigarette lighter. While everyone was busy unwrapping their presents we all suddenly noticed that John was gone. Where could he have disappeared to? After some time he returned, obviously quite winded. It seems that when he received the cigarette lighter from me, he was embarrassed about not having a gift for me. Since most of the stores were closed, he had a hard time finding an open shop where he could make a purchase. He presented me with a pocketknife that had a gold leaf inlay in the handle, and I was very proud of it. Mother, of course, was the first one who caught on to what had happened. She could not suppress her feelings and broke out laughing at the always proper John, for he was always such a perfectionist in everything he did. The family had a good laugh at his expense. It especially made me feel good when, eavesdropping, I heard mother teasing him about the whole episode.

Coming to the bank on Monday morning, we noticed that a definite gloom had come over the personnel. Everybody looked sad. We felt that they were all staring at us as we entered. Then one of the tellers motioned for me to come to his window.

"Paulusha," he whispered, "something terrible has happened. Your friend Kolya went swimming in the Kuban River yesterday. He was overcome with cramps and drowned." I stared at him for a moment, then ran back into the archive room to cry. He had been like a brother to me and would be hard to replace.

A new boy came to fill the position. His name was Petya. This boy was just the opposite from Kolya. He was greedy and ill-tempered. Instead of cooperating, he insisted upon competing. Not only did we indulge in arguments, but often we had fistfights. It took a while to get adjusted to one another before we were able to get into mischief together.

Our favorite pastime was to get out on the balcony on the street side and harass the pedestrians. We made lassos with ordinary string and competed in dropping them over people passing underneath. Some of the passerby looked up and good-naturedly smiled, but others resented it and complained to the doorman--"the admiral," as we called him, because of his gold-braided uniform. He then took delight in scolding us and on occasion even reported us to the bank president, Berberow. That doorman delighted in picking on us. He even resented it when we came sliding down the banister--which was for us much faster than coming down step by step.

We had a desk to ourselves. Sometimes having nothing to do, we would compete in forging the various signatures. My specialty was the signature of the president. It looked almost exactly like his.

One day the fiery Armenian walked close to our desk and paused for a moment to investigate the nature of our deskwork. To his surprise, he found his signature written many times on a piece of paper. That was so serious that he had us both march into his office. He lectured us about signing and imitating someone else's name. He said that it was a crime and could land either of us in jail or even send us to Siberia. He concluded with the remark that if he ever caught either of us practicing forging a name again, we would immediately be fired.

One of the most generous tippers was a tobacco millionaire named Trachow. He asked me on one occasion to deliver a telegram for him. I told him that I would have to get the president's permission. Permission granted, I reached the street just as his coachman arrived to pick him up. Trachow called, "Paulusha, come on. I'll give you a lift part of the way." I jumped on the coach and sat down beside him. I was thrilled to sit beside a millionaire, swiftly driving down the street. I felt important; suddenly those people on the sidewalk were beneath me. I actually felt like a millionaire. It was something I would be able to brag about for a long time.

Krasnodar was a lively city. It had beautiful parks and places of amusement. One could go to a museum, a picture gallery, or several theaters. On Sundays, the main attraction was the activities in the city park. Then a *cossack* band was giving a concert. If one did not care for music, one could walk a short distance away and watch the soccer game.

The main street, *Krasnaya Uliza* (Red Street), was so crowded with promenaders every Saturday and Sunday night that if one wanted to make headway, one had to get off the sidewalk and walk on the street.

Some of my friends persuaded me to enroll in a night school. John was pleased when he heard of my decision. At least I would be making an effort to improve myself. At the same time he was a bit worried about the company I would be getting into. There was always the danger that I might join a gang and get into serious trouble. That possibility was by no means remote. His fears were not groundless. Coming from the well-supervised village life, I was rather innocent. Soon I was a member of a group that delighted in having its main activities after school hours. It soon became clear to me that the school was just a convenient way to meet. The main goal was to roam around the city until midnight. Lining up in front of a theater ticket window, the leader of the gang would step up and ask the cashier whether we could get in for ten kopeks apiece. The cashier, usually a lady, then stuck her head out and looked over the crowd and said, "You may." All of us would file by and hand her the ten kopeks. Whether the cashier let us in at such a reduced price out of compassion or out of fear was not quite clear to us.

Our favorite pictures, of course, were the American cowboy films. The French comedian Max Linder was a favorite.

Sometimes about midnight I would become suspicious and look around toward the entrance. Then I would see brother John, standing and craning his neck to locate his younger brother. A scene at home was the natural thing to expect. As much as I admired my brother, when he proceeded to lecture me I resented it-- it meant he was trying to assume father's place, and no one, but no one, could do that.

It was not that I had the desire to become a hooligan; I simply had to be active. If father had lived, things would have been different. He always spoke of one day sending me to a military school; but as things turned out, John was the only one permitted to get a good education. This I was beginning to throw up to him, and it was painful for both him and mother.

Most of my friends were proud of their homemade zip guns that we called "Monte Cristos." It was a status symbol to have one of them made by one's own hands. I started to whittle a stalk and fasten the empty rifle shell in position. Before I got much farther my conscience stopped me. I began to think of what father would say about my actions. I threw the thing away and quit the gang and the night school. Home training had triumphed and saved me from possible misfortune, and I was glad.

On a Saturday afternoon mother

gave me some money and asked me to
do the marketing for her since she had
to attend a meeting at the church. At
the entrance to the market I saw people
gathered around in a circle watching
something. I had to investigate. It
was a man with a little stand in front
on him playing the shell game. People
paid their money and took chances to
pick the shell that hid the pellet. Some
of them won, but not many. Those that
lost were not watching the gambler's
hands closely enough--so I thought.
To me it seemed fairly simple to watch
his movements, not realizing that the
pellet would not be under any of the
shells. I took a chance. Mother
would be proud to have me double
her money for her. Why not? I put
my money on the stand and told the
man to move the shells. Already I
could envision myself as a lucky
winner. I was stunned. The shell
that I touched hid no pellet. How
could that be? I had lost my

mother's shopping money. Ashamed and crestfallen, I stumbled toward home, crying all the way. Sobbing, I blurted out my crime the minute mother came home. To my surprise, she neither scolded nor uttered a harsh word, but instead said, "I am glad you lost, Son. It has taught you never to gamble."

The one thing stressed in our family was never to lie to our parents. Mother took rather unfair advantage, knowing that I would never tell her a lie. So sometimes out of the blue she would ask:

"Paul. When did you smoke last?" Now, that would always put me on the spot no matter how carefully I concealed the fact. She knew how to check up on me. What a secret agent she would have made!

Despite the fact that I had to stand for a lot of teasing by my gambling experience, I eventually lived it down and tried to make up the loss to mother by turning more of my tip money over to her.

Sister Rosalia, who was now old enough to do some teasing herself, sometimes saw to it that when I returned home to my room I would find three half walnut shells on my bed. She would be standing behind the door to see my reaction to her little prank.

Every morning on my way to the bank I would first accompany Rosalia to her school. She had to cross a marketplace, and mother was always afraid that something might happen to her. One morning she was not her cheerful self. I asked her if she did not feel good and she nodded her head. I touched her forehead, and it felt hot. We immediately returned home. Fortunately, brother was still at home. He rushed her to the hospital, which was only three blocks away. The attending doctor diagnosed her illness as scarlet fever.

The health authorities came and fumigated our house. They had windows and doors tightly sealed and burned some evil-smelling sulphur compound. It had to be done to avoid quarantine.

During sister's confinement I always stopped for a few moments to visit with her. One had to talk through a window. Physical contact was not permitted. My visits were always cut short because I abhorred funerals and being with sick people. When mother came to see her, she asked Rosalia whether Paul had come to see her, and Rosalia answered, "Yes, he was here, but he never stays long." In the meantime, I had saved up some money to buy her a homecoming present. It was a complete toy kitchen set--stove, table, chairs, and dishes--to play with when she got home.

Coming home one day I noticed that something was afoot. I always had to pass the kitchen door to enter the house, and mother would always have something to say. But this day she was quiet and pretended not to notice me. Coming into the dining room, I saw the reason for this mysterious behavior. Little sister was standing in front of the window with her back turned toward me, pretending likewise, not to have noticed my coming in. Her long hair hung down over her shoulders, almost reaching her hips. She had her kitchen set up and was playing house. The whole thing was a conspiracy! Mother and John had the whole thing planned. They knew how close Rosalia and I were and made the most of it. As for me, I started to cry, the most natural thing for me to do, whether out of sadness or out of joy. Father once said, "If that boy ever gets married and his wife spills a glass of milk, he will cry!" Well, we embraced and were happy to be together again.

Scarlet fever often has or leaves some side effects. In Rosalia's case it was losing her hair. It started to fall out. Mother decided that the only way to prevent her from going bald was to have her head shaved. The job was left to John. Poor little sister. It was not enough that she had to walk around with a Mother Hubbard headpiece. There was now her brother Paul, who had something to play with. Fortunately, she was a good little sport when I tried to autograph her skull with an indelible pencil or draw some crude cartoon on it. Occasionally I would spit in the palm of my hand and, striking her on the top of the head, pretend to tell her fortune by the direction the saliva would fly. That would cause her to complain and would always bring mother into the act.

John became increasingly worried about me. He tried to interest me in some kind of a profession or trade, constantly asking me what I would like to be. It was impossible for him to get a serious answer from me. One day I would tell him that slicing sausages would be an easy job, and so why not become a butcher? The next time I would say that I had observed a tailor sitting in a window sewing on buttons, and that was something I could very well handle. All he could do was shake his head and walk away.

Humor with a twist of sarcasm was my defense against everything. Yet at the same time I was proud of John, if he only didn't try to play father to me.

The only thing that saved me from succumbing to bad influences was our tightly knit family and that angel, mother, I always felt sitting on my shoulder.

Brother gained rapid promotion in the bank and was making a good deal more money; thus he was much more able to take care of us. He never showed the least inclination to get married. In retrospect, I believe he must have given father a deathbed promise that he would take care of the family, for that was his entire concern. He was a person who could keep something like that to himself. As for me, I did not have a worry. I just liked to live.

Mother always encouraged me to read good books. Two that I particularly remember were *The Centurian under the Cross* and Bunyan's *Pilgrim's Progress*. Then one day she handed me a book written by a Chinese missionary. Reading it, I was overcome with compassion and pity. Unwittingly I made the remark that I would like to become a missionary. I had struck a match and saw how mother's eyes lit up. She pounced on that remark like a cat on a mouse: "You could make no greater choice nor make your life more useful than serving the Lord" was her response. From that moment on the campaign was on to keep me thinking about the ministry. During a lighter moment she even related a prophecy that one of our former neighbors had made.

One of mother's pet roosters had died, and I thought it deserved a Christian burial. Having taken the dead bird back to the fruit orchard, I dug a hole, placed the bird in it, and proceeded with the burial ritual. The grave covered, a wooden cross was put in place. Praying over the grave as well as pronouncing the benediction, I went on my way. All the while this solemn service took place the spying eyes of the neighbor were watching. He was so impressed that he had to come over and tell my parents that from what he had observed he was convinced we had a preacher in the family. He remarked, "You mark my word, someday that boy is going to be a pastor." When I saw, from day to day, the sparkle that came to mother's eyes whenever she spoke of the ministry, I knew that the die had been cast--it would have to be the ministry.

When John heard about the plan, he, too, was delighted; not so much over my choice (for he was not much of a churchgoer), but over the mere fact that I had finally decided to do something with my life. He lost no time in contacting several seminaries, including one in Switzerland. The answer from every institution was encouraging, but they all suggested that I wait until I had reached the age of eighteen. To wait another three years seemed too long. Mother had another inspiration-- America. She wrote to Uncle Fred, who was a minister in Calgary, Canada. The answer that she received was most encouraging. He wrote that, since he had a family of ten, one more would not make much difference, and he would be only too happy to help. He mentioned that the German Congregational people ran a seminary in Redfield, South Dakota, which eventually I could attend. The first two years I would have to attend public school, and thereafter would be accepted into the preparatory school in Redfield. From then on it would take seven more years to graduate from the seminary. The theology course itself was a three-year course.

The news made me delirious with joy. I was floating on a cloud. *America*--that magic name to every German-Russian, where so many had found happiness and freedom. What boy would not want to go to a land of milk and honey?

Brother John related the news to Pastor Kludt, and in him mother had another ally. He congratulated me and heartily approved. Attending the confirmation class on Saturdays,

I received special attention from then on. For me there was no more turning back. As for my little sister, I had already become a minister; she kept referring to me as "the pastor."

The question remaining was, Where was the money to come from to pay for my passage? To my great surprise and chagrin, who should step forward and offer to advance the money but my old adversary, grandfather Belz. I felt somehow ashamed having misjudged him so; he did have a heart after all. I could not make myself believe that he was advancing the money just to get me out of the country; there must have been some affection motivating his generosity. Perhaps the fact that he did not have the outgoing demonstrative personality of my father had made me misjudge him.

Now things started to progress at a fast pace. John soon had the necessary papers, and of course was getting my traveling kit ready. Mother got me a suitcase woven out of reed, which I jokingly referred to as my "Moses basket" and started to fill it with necessities. She had enough handkerchiefs and socks to last me for a long, long time. It was also her great concern that I should be kept warm; so she made me a red quilt that was to be with me my entire life. Through all the years this quilt has been a symbol of her love.

## Chapter 8
### AMERICA, HERE I COME!

WHEN THE BANK EMPLOYEES heard that Paulusha was going to migrate to America, they all came forth with their congratulations and good wishes. Some of them suggested that I forget about school and just concentrate on marrying a millionaire's daughter and sit back and let others work for me. All wanted to be remembered after I had made my millions.

Pettja wished that he could come along and made me promise that I write just as soon as I had met some cowboys and Indians. They were always the main attractions in the movie houses.

The memorable day of departure came, August 16, 1913. I looked into the face of my mother. The sparkle that was so often evident whenever she spoke of my becoming a minister was not there; there was only sadness. I was unable to understand why she was so sad. After all, it was her wish coming true. I had no conception of what could go on in a mother's heart, when she was seeing her son leave home for a distant land, not knowing whether she would ever see him again. It was not until many years later, when I was able to look into the faces of my own off-spring, that I fully realized and understood her tormented heart.

I was happy and excited. The closest I came to tears was when I put my arms around my baby sister to kiss her good-bye. She was only seven years old. Her big, soulful eyes were overflowing, and tears hung like diamonds on her cheeks. She clung to me as if she had to make one last and final effort to keep her brother at home. I would feel those tiny arms around my neck the rest of my life. I can also remember what sister Maria said: "Mama, how can you send your son into a strange country? Don't you know that you will never see him again?"

How prophetic that statement was! But mother, despite her heavy heart, knew what she was doing. For one thing, she remembered that when father came back from his last trip abroad, he had made the remark that Europe was facing a world war in the near future. The military preparations that he had seen in Germany and Austria clearly pointed in that direction. For mother, sending me away had a twofold purpose. It would prepare me for a useful life and at the same time remove me from all danger. Even John, who should have been rejoicing over the fact that he had one less mouth to feed, was not happy and looked sadder than I had ever seen him. He had decided to accompany me on my trip as far as Bremen, then return home via Switzerland

and Austria.

The reed basket with the red quilt strapped on top was ready. A coach was summoned to take us all to the station. We did not have to wait for my train; it was already on the tracks in front of the station. Mother, with her shawl (my last gift) around her shoulders, held on to my arm; and sister Rosalia, on my other side, held on to my hand. A shrill conductor's whistle and the call "All aboard" was the signal for passengers to line up. One last tearful embrace.

John led the way, and I followed close behind him. I hurried over to the window and stuck my head out for a few last words. Fighting back the tears, I tried hard not to break down, thus making it harder for my loved ones. A loud blast from the locomotive's steam whistle, and our train jerked into motion. The door between my family and me had closed forever. We kept waving to each other until finally the statue of grief and sorrow, supported by her two daughters, disappeared from sight-- I was on my way to the Promised Land!

Our first stop was Rostov on the Don. Here we had to change trains. John decided we would stay there overnight. Our former bank president, Berberow, had in the meantime accepted a job in the Rostov bank, and brother was anxious to pay him a visit.

The fiery Armenian was happy to see us. He especially remembered my skill as a forger; and when he learned that I was on my way to America, he, like the others, came up with the remark "So Paulusha wants to become a millionaire?" It seemed that the mere name of America immediately suggested wealth.

The result of our visit was that John was offered a promotion with a considerable raise in salary if he would come to the Rostov bank. Of course, brother gladly accepted. It had made us both feel very happy. I knew that upon returning home, mother and Rosalia had the pleasant surprise coming, that they, too, would soon be ready to move.

Rostov was a bigger city than Krasnodar. While Krasnodar had only a few buildings higher than two stories, Rostov had many buildings as many as ten stories high. These tall buildings fascinated me; and because my eyes were always cast upward, I kept bumping into people, which to my perfectly mannered brother was embarrassing. He admonished me slightly and told me to watch where I was going.

Suddenly I came to an abrupt stop. What brother's warning had not accomplished an iron lamppost did. I had walked into one, and for a moment I had a number of luminous objects floating in front of my eyes; and I had to hold on to the post to keep from falling over. The impact had raised quite a lump on my forehead. Every time brother looked at me, he had to chuckle. I found it much easier from then on to watch my steps. This lesson, that lampposts had to be avoided, stayed with me.

Our next stop was Warsaw. Here, too, we had to wait for a few hours and took the time to walk to the center of the city. The station was one of the most beautiful I had ever seen. The floor was of tiny inlaid mosaic tiles.

Downtown it almost seemed that every other male that we passed on the street wore a long black coat and a small skullcap. Brother explained that they were Orthodox Jews.

After a few hours we were again back on the train and heading for our next stop Berlin.

Crossing the East Prussian border,

I was impressed by the remarkable order and cleanliness apparent everywhere. As far as the eye could see, plots of ground were orderly laid out and planted with various kinds of grain and vegetation. Nothing was wasted. The countryside looked like a great big patchwork quilt. It was apparent that cleanliness was a fetish with these people.

When we arrived in Berlin, we saw the same cleanliness and order. The streets looked as if they had just been scrubbed. We could not help but remember how father had described the various cities he had visited. Paris, he said, was the most beautiful, Rome the most interesting, Vienna the most exciting, and Berlin the cleanest. We stayed in Berlin only two days. We took a walk *unter den Linden* and visited the Sieges Allée, where we saw the statues of all the German men of history. We also drove by the

Reichstag amd Kaiser Hoff.

On the third day we left for Hamburg. Here we stayed about a week. Our hotel became overcrowded, so much so that the clerk asked us whether we would permit one of the guests to sleep in our room--just for one night. Brother consented. The gentleman who was to be our guest was well dressed and apparently well educated. That night, as we retired and the lights were turned out, I asked our brother in an audible whisper (not realizing that Austrians, too, spoke German), "Have you put the money in a safe place?" From across the room came a response from our guest in flawless German: "Young man, have no fear. I am not after your money."

For a moment there was complete silence. But for one who could extract humor from any kind of situation, this was simply too overpowering to keep me silent. I could not contain myself and burst out laughing. Brother and the Austrian joined in. It was quite a while before I had my last "chuckle."

Hamburg was definitely the high point of our trip. We visited all the museums, picture galleries, and aquariums. We also took a cruise down the river and generally had a wonderful time together. Before we left the city brother bought me a picture album with the inscription "To my dear brother Paul, in memory of the wonderful days spent in Hamburg-- from your brother John."

That album is now an antique but still in good condition.

At last we arrived at our final destination, Bremerhaven. Here would be out last and final parting. I would board the ship, and he would take the train to Switzerland. He gave me some last-minute advice and handed me a piece of paper with my itinerary clearly marked. Because he was such a perfectionist, everything went according to his schedule: "When you get to New York, send this telegram (he had written it out) to Uncle Fred; it tells him when you will arrive in Calgary, so that somebody will meet you at the station."

Walking up the gangplank with all my worldly possessions on my shoulder in a reed basket, I had the feeling that I was crossing a bridge from one world into another. As I stood on board and looked at my brother, the distance already seemed a thousand miles. The sailors hauled in the heavy anchor ropes, the raucous blast of the steam whistle was the signal that it was time to shove off. The ship, *Koenig Albert*, started to move and headed for the open sea.

I saw my brother walking along the dock, keeping pace with the ship as long as was possible, waving his hat. The distance between shore and ship now kept increasing. I still could see my brother waving his Tyrolean hat, and I waved back. We were saying good-bye for the last time, and it had to be prolonged. Finally the curtain fell.

After the last vestige had vanished and there was nothing but sky and sea, the feeling of being alone hit me, and I broke down sobbing. Even though weeping had always been easy for me, this was different. These tears came from an inner pain I had not known before. It was as if the floodgates had broken open, releasing every tear within me. That painful moment was also a blessing. I had become a man; a complete metamorphosis had taken place in a very short time. I realized that from then on the pilot wheel of my life would be in my own hands; there would be no more depending on John and mother.

We were now on the high seas. The waves were tossing the boat as if it were a toy. A school of playful dolphins appeared and formed a convoy. They kept jumping in and out of the water, easily keeping up with the ship. It seemed that they had a lot of fun doing it. Like a group of clowns, they kept entertaining the passengers and cheering them on their way to a new homeland.

For many of the passengers the interest in the dolphins was of short duration, for they suddenly found themselves preoccupied with something quite unexpected. They started to make hurried trips to the ship's railing. It was as if there were a contest going on in trying to beat one another to the side. Lips pressed tightly together and cheeks bulging like those of a tuba player, they presented quite a sight as they heaved their rejected stomach cargo overboard. The steerage compartment was the worst. Here some of the victims could not or would not start running in time and would

deposit the slimy mess right
beside their cots or on the floor
as they tried to reach the top.
The floors got to be slippery,
and the sailors began to curse
the untidy housekeepers. There
was nothing that could be done.

For some reason I had attracted
the attention of one of the officers.
He came over to me and asked
me whether I would be interested
in occupying his cabin during the
night for a small fee, since he was
on night duty and could let me
have it. I was only too happy to
get away from that steerage
"skating rink" and pay him the
nightly fee of two marks.

Standing near the ship's railing
and looking down, watching the
swelling waves as they lifted the
ship up and down, I felt a slight
tapping on my shoulder. One
of the sailors had observed me
and said that looking down into

the water was the surest way
to get seasick. This was one
bit of advice I did not heed and
so also became a "tuba player."

On the eighth day we heard the
magic call: "Land ho!" We were at
last approaching New York harbor.
The huge skyscrapers appearing on
the horizon had everyone breathless.
The closer we came, the more
hypnotic the vision. The climax
came when we passed the lady
holding high the torch, lighting our
way, and bidding welcome to
children soon to be adopted. Some
of the passengers could hardly wait
to embark and go on an exploring
trip. I was attracted by some
stevedores unloading fresh fruit
from a freighter anchored nearby.
They all were happy at their work,
and it looked as if they were playing.
The work was a game to them.

As I watched, one of the men dropped a crate of oranges. I could not tell whether it was an accident or a deliberate act. The oranges were rolling in every direction over the deck. Then it started. They were all laughing and throwing oranges at each other. I felt good watching these grown-up children at play. To me it symbolized the character of America, and I was glad I had come.

Even though thousands of miles away from home, in a land whose people spoke a different language, I was totally without fear. People all acted as if they were related to each other--as indeed they were. They all belonged to that wonderful family, America.

On board ship I had gotten to know a Polish family by the name of Bukowski. They, too, were destined for Canada. Somehow they got the impression that I knew where I was going and always kept following my lead. If I reached for my basket to pack, they would follow suit. I merely followed the instructions my brother had written for me on a piece of paper, but the Bukowskis followed me.

At Ellis Island I sent my telegram to Uncle Fred in Calgary, informing him of the exact date of my arrival. What uncle thought of my time schedule we shall find out a little later.

We were told to line up in front of the food dispensary. By paying two dollars we each received a food package. It contained several cans of sardines, some sandwiches, a few hard-boiled eggs, and an apple pie. The pie was something new to me and received first attention; it was my first American act. I liked it very much.

A uniformed man had us line up in the proper groups. Our baggage was checked by the customs official. That done, we were herded toward our particular coach. My group, destined for Canada, was loaded into a Pullman coach that was also a smoker. The unfamiliar odor of American cigarettes at first was rather repulsive, but after a while even preferable to the smell of Turkish tobacco. We were now on our way to the interior of our new homeland. The faces were pressed against the windows. No one wanted to miss a thing, and each thought that he had to call everyone's attention to what he saw. There was continuous aisle-hopping going on--we wanted to see both sides. America, we are going to like you!

Unfortunately, we soon had to learn that not all people in this Promised Land were angels. One such an obnoxious character was the news vendor. This creature came into the coach throwing boxes of chocolate candies on the seats or in one's lap. Some of the immigrants, thinking that it was just another gesture of the country to make everybody welcome, lost no time in sampling the sweets. To me it was not quite believable that handing out chocolate candy was included as a welcoming gift. I let mine lie on the seat beside me untouched. The candy man came back with his basket practically empty, only this time he held out his open palm. Some of them looked sheepish but dug out the money to pay; but others, who had thought it was a gift, shook their heads and refused. Then I saw something that made my blood boil, strange country or not. This man had the nerve to pick up a box and slap one of those foolish people across the face and again demand payment. There was nothing he could do but come up with the money. He approached my seat. I got up, took the box of candy, and threw it into his basket. He looked at me for a moment, bug-eyed, then backed away, muttering, "OK OK!" He obviously did not realize that he had met someone who came from a revolution-minded family. Some of the other immigrants followed my example, at least those who had not opened their boxes, and just laughed at the man as he hastily left the coach.

After the enterprising businessman had left, I felt somebody who was sitting behind me patting my shoulder, saying "That a boy!" I turned and saw the smiling face of the American who was smoking those offensive cigarettes. What he said in English was so near the German that I clearly understood the phrase of approval. I had made my first friend. It nullified my temporary disappointment.

The immigrants in the coach were now in a good mood. One of them had defied injustice and had been supported by an American. It made them all feel a bit bolder.

On the next stop my friend left us. He shook hands with me and said, "Good-bye and good luck!" I was sorry to see him leave. The seat he had vacated was immediately filled by two young men. They conversed with each other in English, but their appearance suggested to me that they were of Slavic descent. I asked them whether they understood Russian, and they responded in the affirmative. I was glad to have found new friends and shared my basket of food with them.

The next morning when I awoke I found my friends gone and with them the rest of my food. While this was another disappointment, I was, however, not surprised. In the country of the Czar, stealing, for the peasant, was almost a necessity. As the saying goes, "A wolf will shed his fur but never his habits." My mind went back to the time when we lived by the mill. I remembered how sometimes while eating supper we would hear the muffled squealing of a piglet that was no doubt being carried away into the dark. No one even bothered to get up from the table and investigate. It was just taken for granted that some hungry peasant was desperate.

Trying to rationalize away my disappointing experiences, I kept peering out the window with the hope of seeing something that would be more uplifting and would nullify and contradict the disappointments.

As we were rolling along I noticed that none of the houses had shutters. Apparently the windows of the homes here did not have to be covered and bolted shut during the nights. Those houses that did have shutters had them only as decorations. I found myself continually making comparisons. Still, I was glad I had come.

With all my food gone, I was becoming

extremely hungry and desperate. We had reached the Canadian border. After crossing the border and coming to our first stop, I noticed a Chinese store close to the station. By using a combination of the Russian and German languages, plus sign language, I was able to make the brakeman understand that I wished to know how many minutes we would be stopping. He held up five fingers, indicating the number of minutes. I bolted toward the store. Almost breathless, I kept repeating, "Bread, bread." The amused Oriental brought me thread. I pointed toward my open mouth, pretending to bite off my finger and chew it, and again repeated, "Bread." Now the light went on. The Chinaman had a wide grin. Bowing, he said, "Ah, so--bled." My life was saved. I ran back to the train, tearing into the loaf as I ran. I sat on the steps of the coach, and by the time the train started to move again, I had devoured almost the entire loaf. It was truly a meal fit for a king! The Russians have a proverb: "Hunger is the best cook." The trip over the Canadian prairie was fascinating. There were so many signs to read. Sounding them out phonetically, I tried to guess their meaning. On the third day the brakeman came through the coach, shouting, "Calgary! Calgary!"

I could feel my heart pounding. Was it really true that within a short time I would meet my second family? My reed basket with the red quilt strapped on to it stood ready. The brakeman, noticing my impatience, held up his hand, indicating the number of minutes that we still had before reaching the station. As soon as the train screeched to a halt, I was the first one out on the platform to set foot on Canadian soil. But where were my relatives? Didn't uncle receive my telegram? There was no one there to meet me.

The proper thing for me to do under the circumstances would have been to sit down inside the station and wait, but that would have required patience, a virtue within me notoriously absent.

There was not a horse in sight.

Apparently they had no horse-drawn carriages, but only motorized cabs. Having only twenty-seven dollars left, and that stashed away inside the stocking under the instep of my left foot, I was not about to remove my shoe for a cab fare. There had to be another way. I picked up my baggage and walked towards town. Coming to the first intersection, I saw a policeman directing traffic. I dug up the slip of paper with uncle's address on it that brother had given me, marched up to the policeman, and held it under his nose. He guessed what I wanted and pointed to a streetcar that happened to be arriving. Walking over, he exchanged a few words with the motorman and motioned for me to get on. Again the slip of paper had to do the talking for me as I held it up to the motorman. He smiled and nodded. Standing directly behind him, I would remind him every so often by holding the card in front of him to make sure he had not forgotten about me. He always nodded and reassured me. Then, coming to a stop, he turned. With a wide grin on his face, he indicated that I was to get off. I was in a residential section at the foot of some hills.

Now, how would I find my uncle's house? Two men came walking across the street. They were definitely German-Russians, as a matter of fact, unmistakably Volga-Germans. I spoke to them in German, and they answered, "You are the nephew that the minister is expecting. We are members of your uncle's church." The man who did most of the talking was a Mr. Knaus, who in later years also studied for the ministry. He proceeded to give me directions how to find the parsonage.

"You see that shack down at the end of the street just on the foot of the hill?" I nodded but had no idea what the word *shack* meant. Since the word sounded like the German *Sheck*, meaning a spotted horse, or a pinto. I gathered that since the tar paper on the outside of that building at the foot of the hill was torn, showing the white boards in different places, that that was the "spotted hut" referred to; and, of course, I was right.

"Well," he continued, "the parsonage is just across from it."

I thanked them, picked up my burden, and started for the house. As I approached the shack, I noticed children playing alongside the hill. One little girl looked my way and gave out a loud cry: "Cousin Paul is here." What a wonderful, wonderful sound that was! I had finally reached my second home. The girls came running over to me. The eight-year old, Bertha, who had announced my arrival, took me by the hand and led me to the door. The children even tried to help me carry my luggage--the most wonderful welcoming committee I could have wished for. Answering the door was Aunt Rose. She definitely favored mother and, still more, grandmother. After the embrace, she apologized for not having had anyone meet me at the station. She explained that according to Uncle Fred's calculations, I was not to arrive until a day later. He remarked, "What does the boy know about train schedules?"

Uncle just did not know my brother. Had

he known him, he would have met the train. Naturally the first hours were spent in asking and answering questions.

Toward evening my uncle came home. His face was red with embarrassment when he saw the Russian nephew had found his home without assistance. He, too, was very apologetic and kept repeating his apology several times during the evening. We all were happy. The oldest cousin, Paul, and Frida were both attending Redfield College in South Dakota. What a family! When everyone was home, including uncle's sister, who stayed with them, we were a family of twelve around the dinner table. No wonder he had written that one more in the family wouldn't make much difference.

## Chapter 9
## PUBLIC SCHOOL IN CANADA

THE TWO LITTLE COUSINS, Bertha, eight, and Hulda, six, had appointed themselves as my tutors. They brought out their school books and proceeded to teach me the alphabet. How surprised they both looked when I picked up one of their readers and proceeded to read it fluently, though, of course, mispronouncing a lot of words. The little one asked, "How come you can read such a funny English?"

I had to explain to them that in the Russian-German school we had to learn Russian and German, and also read the Latin script, and that the English language used Latin letters. They later bragged to the other children that their cousin was able to read three different languages.

After a few day's rest, uncle took me to the nearest public school and enrolled me. It was the Riverside Grade School, where all the rest of the cousins were attending, five in all. There was one in almost every grade up to the seventh.

Hulda came home happy because Paul was in her class. Since my problem was not the language, the teacher in the first grade had the most time to spare. For me there was only one problem--how to fit my almost six-foot frame into one of those tiny desks. By throwing my foot over so that I had a leg in either aisle, I managed to squeeze in, holding the desk, as it were, between my legs.

The teacher appreciated my predicament and devoted a lot of time to teaching me vocabulary. She no doubt was anxious to pass me on as soon as possible. She could also see that instead of being embarrassed, I liked and enjoyed the company of children. It was quite a problem to keep them away from my desk. Every once in a while one of them would leave his or her desk to come over and try to help me. They no doubt thought I was some kind of a retarded person that needed assistance. The teacher repeatedly had to order them back to their desks, explaining over and over again that I was there only to learn the language.

There was a loud protest in the classroom the day my teacher announced that Paul was ready to move to a higher grade. My progress was fairly rapid.

Uncle and aunt were delighted at the progress I was making. They really succeeded in making me feel that I was an adopted son. In every way I was treated the same as the rest of the family except I was spared the criticism and harsh words sometimes directed at them.

Cousin Theo was my age but not quite as tall. Uncle wisely would always take us shopping together and buy us suits quite similar to make sure I would not feel any discrimination.

At the end of the first year I had passed three of the cousins, and now was in Alma's class. Alma was thirteen. "Paul," uncle remarked one day, "you have passed all of them except Theo. I don't think you will catch him."

Uncle had several rural churches. The first summer he got jobs for both of us where we could earn a few dollars during the summer months. The farmer who hired me was one of his deacons. He had a family of four, all well-behaved children. They accepted me as a big brother and made me feel very much at home. The father, however, was a disappointment. The first feature that impressed me was his cruelty toward his stock. He delighted to use the whip and even a pitchfork on them. One day a white-faced bull broke through the fence to join some cattle on the open range. The deacon armed himself with a fork and rode out to bring the animal back. While chasing the bull, he kept jabbing him with the fork, so that by the time they arrived in the yard the animal's flanks and rump were a bloody mess. While jabbing the beast, he kept hissing, "I'll teach you to stay in your own yard!" This Sunday Christian delighted in working me like an animal. He simply was a sadist who liked to see man and beast suffer.

Every morning after breakfast he would dig out the Bible and read a portion of Scripture, following it with a lengthy prayer. He was sure that the Lord would give his blessing for the day ahead.

"So you want to become a preacher? Well, I'll show you what it means to work for a living." And that was the beginning of a day.

By the end of the day I was hardly able to lift my arms. Blisters as big as small coins appeared in the palms of my hands, which merely delighted him. My whole body was in pain. Tossing and turning, I could not find a relaxing position in which to rest.

The first day out on the field, plowing, I kept staring down, watching the earth turn over and listening to the sound of tearing roots. I was hypnotized into a nostalgic trance. I was back spending happy days roaming around the mill in Russia. I thought of mother and the rest of my family. If only mother could see me now. And for the second time since leaving home, I broke down sobbing.

The boss kept tantalizing and teasing me daily without letup. It seemed to irk him that I had come from the city.

One day we were out stacking hay. I was on top of the haystack to keep the sides nice and straight while he was manning the sweep that brought the hay upon the lifting fork on the stacker. Now, to cause embarrassment for me, this fiend first of all created piles very close to the haystack in order to save time by not going out in the field after it. That would not give the man on the stack enough time. So he would keep on dumping one load after another on the stack, not giving me time enough to arrange the hay properly--just to see how fast he could completely cover me up. I was getting angrier by the minute. Finally I had had enough. The next load that came sliding up I met with my fork before it slid off unto the stack and with a hard push sent it back to him again. This impudence on my part made him furious. He threatened to use a fork handle on me. I challenged him to come right ahead. He decided otherwise.

The end of my endurance came one day when he again came out to check on my work. It so happens that when one is plowing virgin soil sometimes brush roots or rocks will cause the plow to jump out, thus missing a spot where the soil has not been properly turned over. He kept nagging me about these spots. As he was lecturing me, one of the horses, a stallion, kept bothering the horse next to him. That angered him so that he broke a piece of board from a nearby fence and hit the animal across the nose. I noticed that the stallion kept shaking his head and chewing his bit in an unusual manner. I stepped over to investigate. Lifting the animal's upper lip, I saw an ugly wound and the mouth running over with blood. Apparently, a nail in the board had penetrated all the way through. I said to him, "Look what you have done! You are a monster, and I cannot work for you any longer." With that I stomped off the field, leaving him standing with his chin sagging, utterly stunned. All he could do was manage a feeble call after me: "You can't do that!" I could and did.

When I came home unexpectedly and explained to my uncle and aunt why I had to quit my job, they both were sympathetic. My uncle even said to me, "Having known your father, that would have been exactly what he would have done." Continuing, he looked at Aunt Rose and remarked, "Just like Gottlieb!"

Within a few days he had another job lined up for me with another farmer to serve out the rest of the summer.

When I came back to Calgary to attend the second year in school, Cousin Theo was transferred to the junior high school (Central High) while I stayed at Riverside. This second year progress came much easier for me. Having acquired a conversational vocabulary I was advanced to the eighth grade and also joined Theo at Central.

Our teacher took great interest in athletics and persuaded us to enroll in the school cadet corps. The military training was very much to my liking. We were issued

Springfield rifles with which to train. I got a little taste of the course I would have pursued had not my father died so early in life.

One day our teacher invited us to come with him to the gymnasium to watch a boxing match. There was a ring roped off, and two of the upper classmates had "a go" at each other. Our seats were very close to the ring, I must have shown a bit too much enthusiasm, for I noticed the attention of the referee. One of the participants suddenly removed his gloves and stepped out of the ring. Apparently he had had enough. I noticed the referee summoning my teacher and whispering something while at the same time glancing in my direction. My teacher nodded in agreement. The referee then motioned to me and called out, "Hey, Dutch, come here!" My teacher smiled at me and indicated for me to go ahead. I never in my life had had on a pair of boxing gloves, and would have preferred the bare-knuckle old-country style. But when in Rome one must do as the Romans do. The referee assisted me in putting on the gloves while giving me instructions as to legal and illegal blows. In Russia, when I was in a fight, there was no such thing as an illegal blow. There was only an adversary in front of one that one had to subdue. There was no science--just muscle and temper working for one.

    The gong sounded, and we were to start boxing. My opponent started some fancy footwork which I had not learned. So the dancing had to be a solo. I kept moving about, flatfooted, but watching his hands closely. Before I knew it, I had collected a few jabs in my face. I became increasingly irritated and felt my blood pressure rising. Just about the time he again made the attempt to flick his left in my face, I swung from the floor and, to my surprise, connected. My opponent found himself sitting on the floor. He got up immediately and resumed his dance. Again I was lucky with the same kind of blow, and he went down again. This time he got up and started to take off his gloves and disgustedly remarked, "The Dutchman does not know how to box," and stepped out of the ring.

I looked over in the direction of my teacher and saw him clapping his hands and laughing. Others joined him. The spectators no doubt had anticipated some fun at my expense; but when the game went the other way, they were equally amused and cheered. I had gained recognition plus a nickname that I was unable to shake-- Dutch.

Theo and I graduated from the eighth grade together. On graduation day the school principal called me to the front to meet the district superintendent and announced to the audience that an immigrant boy was able to graduate from the eighth grade after his second year in the country. It was a mystery to me why the fuss. After all, it was primarily the language that was my problem.

The second summer we both again went to work for farmers. This time I was fortunate. It was just the opposite of the previous summer. The man who hired me was a "gentleman farmer," a well-educated Scotsman. His wife was the daughter of a ship's captain. Again there were children in the family, seven-year-old Elsie and two-year-old Johnny. One of my daily chores was to saddle a docile pony for little Elsie and see her off to school in the morning.

I had many cows to milk--a job I did not like. Not used to that kind of work, my hands would always be swollen by the time I finished. But despite that, working for the Dickensons was sheer pleasure. The boss, Bert Dickenson, was, besides being an educated man, somewhat of a clown and was always entertaining. His specialty was imitating Harry Lauder.

When he sang one of those Scottish ballads, he put a burr in his *r's* that would have put a buzz saw to shame. It was a joy to listen to him. He should have been on the stage instead of the farm. Sometimes he would forget himself, so that I had to remind him that we had some work to do-- that always amused him, the hired hand reminding his boss to go to work. He had a slight stutter which made his renditions all the more funny. There was never a dull moment.

The adjoining property was a vast cattle ranch belonging to the well-known meatpacker, Burns.

One day, while clearing away some brush near the fence, I noticed a newborn calf trying to struggle to its feet but never quite being able to make it. I crawled through the wires to be a good Samaritan and help the poor creature. Just as I brought it to its feet, I heard an angry bellow. Looking in its direction, I noticed an animal leaving the herd and trotting towards me. I did not hesitate to find out whether the animal objecting to my good deed was a cow or a bull. What happened next would have been a credit to any Olympic sprinter. I had no desire to get help from a pair of horns to clear the fence. I jumped it with space to spare--and just in time. The angry mother cow had just slid to a stop, the barbed wire between us. She was snorting and pawing the ground. The way she was rolling her eyes conveyed the message to me that in the future I had better stay on my own side of the fence. What I said to that cow could hardly be quoted from a pulpit. But to be safe, I increased the distance between us.

At another time I was out on the field mowing hay. The boss came out to see me. While we were chatting, Bert called my attention to some ominous clouds moving from the south in a northeasterly direction and heading towards us. He suggested that the cloud was coming on fast and that I had better unhitch and head for home. He left right away. Thinking that he was unduly alarmed, I procrastinated. Then I heard a swishing sound, a sound I had never heard before. This could not have been made by rain alone; it was something else. I quickly unhitched the mower, hitched up the wagon, and drove for home at a gallop. Good old Bert. He had had presence of mind to leave the gate and the double barn door open for me. Coming through the gate with my eyes closed most of the time, it was a miracle that I did not hit the posts. Some of the hail stones were the size of chicken eggs and bounced like corn in a giant popper. Coming to a stop inside the barn and looking very scared, I saw my boss standing there, grinning. In his very best Scotsman's brogue, he said, "Din I tell ya to hurrrry?"

I had been lucky to reach the barn before the full fury of the storm hit. It was the most awesome sight that one could ever see. Trees were defoliated, and branches were knocked off. The wheat fields were a total loss. The grain that was almost ready for harvest was literally pounded into the ground. There was not a square inch of soil that was not covered with a blanket of hail and ice. The people all agreed that is was the worst storm they had ever experienced.

Bert had his crop fully insured, but he was not laughing. The only thing to do was to clean up and get ready for the next summer.

Time had come for the new school term. This time it meant Redfield College, Redfield, South Dakota.

The morning I left the Dickensons it reminded me somewhat of my departure from home in Russia. Once more I saddled the pony for little Elsie. She knew I was leaving and put her arms around my neck, kissing me good-bye. For the moment they were not the tiny arms of a little Scottish lass that I felt, but the arms of Rosalia. I shall always remember the Dickensons for the kindness and consideration they showed a lonesome immigrant boy.

## *Chapter 10*
### REDFIELD COLLEGE

THE WAR IN EUROPE WAS in full swing. There was as yet no panic at home. Sister Rosalia kept sending me stories and articles as well as postcard pictures of Russian war heroes, especially of cossacks that had distinguished themselves.

My uncles both were on the fighting front. Uncle Jacob was on the Russo-Prussian front and Uncle John on the Turkish frontier. I never heard from Uncle Jacob directly except for the poems mother sent me that he wrote while in the trenches. Uncle John, however, still knew how to fire a boy's imagination. He would describe in detail, for instance, what happened to him while on sentry duty:

> We were moving in on the fortress of Erzerym. The Turks were retreating and we were in close pursuit.

> One night, as I was on sentry duty,
> a Turkish soldier, a mere boy, came
> upon me. I wanted to take him
> prisoner, but he chose to fight. In
> our hand-to-hand combat, to save
> my own life, I had to run him
> through with my bayonet. I shall
> never forget that boy's face as
> long as I live. At night, when I try
> to sleep, always that boy's face.
> I could not help but imagine his
> mother's grief in learning of her
> son's death. Why must we
> have wars?

Mother's letters were always cheerful. She was happy that her son was out of danger. When she wrote and told me that my closest friend, David Witche, had been killed in action, I had a feeling of deep guilt. Why should my life be spared while my comrades were sacrificing theirs? I wished that I had stayed to face whatever fate was in store for them. It was the type of mood and thinking that still fills the recruiting stations with innocent boys.

Arriving in Redfield, Cousin Theo and I moved into the college dormitory. The school was coeducational and subsidized by the German Congregational Church of America. Most of the male students had come to prepare themselves for the ministry. Obviously, the intent of most of the coeds was becoming ministers' wives. The relationships between men and women were, however, very proper and under strict supervision. It was a reward for any graduating minister to take with him a wife who knew and understood the life she had chosen. Such unions were bound to be blessed and had a definite advantage.

The dormitory for the next seven years was to be my only home. It was an extraordinary piece of good fortune. The students there were friendly and helpful. We were one big family. The pleasant atmosphere of dormitory life helped to dispel the homesickness that was sure to come.

There was always a good deal of mischief

afoot, in which I was a willing participant. It was not uncommon to enter one's room and find everything rearranged to suit someone else's artistic taste. Pictures on the wall would be hanging upside down; table, chairs, and bed rearranged; and bookcases facing the wall. Whenever such redecorating had taken place, detective work had to be done. How else was it possible to retaliate?

There was the unique case of the farmer boy's bibbed overalls. This student came from a farm in Montana. He could not part with his overalls and would wear them even to class. Telling him to conform had no effect. Something had to be done.

One morning, as he got out of bed to slip into his beloved garment, his toes struck a dead end in a gooey mess. Someone had sewn the pant legs shut and poured molasses in each of them. Enraged, our friend picked up his sabotaged garment and went looking for the dean to register his complaint. The dean had already been in his classroom. Since I sat close to the door, I was able to see and partly hear the somewhat excited conversation that went on outside the classroom door. The dean at least pretended to be concerned, and I could hear him say that he would do something about it. Returning to his desk, he looked slightly amused and from time to time would look over in my direction. Naturally I had to show my unusual attendance to my book. The class over, the dean asked me to remain. Telling me what had happened and showing that he enjoyed relating the episode, he asked me, "Would you know anything about it? Montana pointed the finger at you." At that particular time I did not think that "confession was good for the soul" and shook my head. I went immediately to my accuser's room and pleaded innocence, and in turn pointed the finger at his roommate, who actually had been an accomplice. It was he who had smuggled the overalls to us. The other coconspirator was my friend Gross. I persuaded our friend to make a formal charge against his roommate and told him that he would arrange a court trial. He agreed to do so. I also suggested to him that he should pick himself as a prosecuting attorney. He asked me to take the job, and I gladly accepted it.

Having accomplished that much, it only remained to have Gross be the defense counsel, and the stage would be set. That, too, was accomplished. We both had the defendant promise that he would not inform on either of us. So it was that prosecutor and defense attorney were the only ones that knew the whole story--how the pants were taken down to the college kitchen, how the cook was willing to let us use her sewing machine, and how Gross, at the time manager of the boarding club, furnished the molasses.

The court session was called for, and the time was set--every Saturday night. The judge was appointed, a jury of twelve "good and true" were chosen, and the wheels of justice were set in motion. It was the high spot of the week. All the students looked forward to these Saturday night sessions.

Having the two principals in the crime act as prosecution and defense was like "letting a couple of goats guard the cabbage."

The presiding judge continually had to pound for "order in the court" and occasionally threatened to clear the room if the spectators did not refrain from their loud laughter. These court sessions furnished the entertainment for many a Saturday night before the case finally went to jury.

Before the jury had a chance to render its verdict a motion of mistrial was introduced by the defense. The motion was based on jury tampering on the part of the prosecution. It was alleged that the prosecutor had contacted some jury members in secret to gain a favorable verdict and therefore a mistrial should be considered. The judge agreed, and the case was dismissed. All that was accomplished was good entertainment that was to be the talk of the dormitory for some time to come.

The aftermath was that the overalls were seen hanging in the gym dressing room for a long time. The molasses in the meantime had crystallized, leaving part of the pants legs quite stiff. Eventually Montana could not wait any longer. He ripped open the seams and soaked his favorite garment in some strong detergent to get rid of the molasses.

Saturday night was also the night of hair tonic and cologne. It was the night for dates when almost every damsel in the ladies' hall, which was off campus, expected her boyfriend to call for her and take in a moving picture show or the Schiller Verein (a literary club taking place in the college chapel).

The entertainment in this club was furnished by the students. The program committee always saw to it that all the students got a turn to participate. One of the most interesting items was always the newscast. Many--and often--embarrassing--secrets were revealed, and students were always apprehensive, waiting to have their names mentioned.

We had a songbook containing patriotic

and popular folk songs. Any member was free to call for his favorite number. My roommate, Edward, always made sure that Bobby Burn's song. "My heart's in the Highlands; my heart is not here," was included. He knew that it was my favorite song and that I often sang it when homesick for the mountains in the Caucasus.

News from Russia became increasingly ominous. Severe restrictions were imposed upon the German-Russian people. The German language was prohibited in schools and church, and religious gatherings were frowned upon by the Soviet government.

After Hindenburg had defeated the Russian army, many soldiers deserted the front and came home to join the revolutionary groups. The long-awaited revolution had come, forcing the Czar to abdicate. It was time for rejoicing.

Brother John and uncle could now sing their revolutionary songs to their hearts' content. The new government, under the leadership of Alexander Kerensky, was, however, of short duration. Another revolution had torn through the country.

The Germans, anxious to get the Russians out of the war, smuggled the exiled Lenin, residing in Switzerland, back into Russia. He had told them that he would take Russia out of the war and conclude a separate peace. This was accomplished, and Lenin became the new head of the government.

A different wind was blowing in the country. The letters I received from home began to sound more pessimistic. When I wrote to John and expressed my enthusiasm by saying that I thought that we in America would soon be envious of them, he wrote back and begged me henceforth to refrain from making political comments. I also received a letter from Uncle John in which he stated, "My dear nephew, I see that you Americans are looking forward to the time when you will envy us. I trust that you are not envying us now, ha, ha." That indicated to me clearly that my people were not happy over the things that were happening.

The clouds over my people became ever darker and more ominous. The village was forced to become *kolchos* (collective farm). The landowners who were reluctant to give up their property were branded "kulack" and people to be despised. Letters reached me heavily censored. Sometimes whole pages had been blotted out. I was beginning to have difficulty sleeping and when I did fall asleep would be tormented by terrible nightmares. My roommate often had to shake me to bring me out of them. The nightmares always had similar characteristics and always involved my mother. I would be coming home for a visit, only to find my mother locked up in a dark room, completely insane, never able to recognize me. So it went night after night.

Students who knew me on the campus as an easygoing, jolly person who had a natural penchant for fun and frivolity could not understand my change of mood. They failed to realize that clowns sometimes are basically sad people. They knew me only as one who always liked to indulge in some harmless practical joke. What they did not know was that I often left my room at midnight to sit out in the grandstand and look up into the starry sky, asking plaintively, "Dear God, why?" while tears moistened my face. Letters from mother clearly revealed what had taken place in our village. People who through the years had been ne'er-do-wells were now the leaders.

Grandfather Belz, due to his age, was considered harmless and permitted to stay in the bunkhouse while his mansion was being turned into a commune hospital.

An outsider by the name of Lemeshkin had been appointed *komissar* and overseer in the village. Not only was it difficult for me to concentrate on my studies, but I had the additional problem of working my way through school. As a self-supporting student, I had no one to rely upon for subsidy. Uncle Fred had helped me the first two years but was not able to assist me any longer. Cousin Theo even returned home and gave up school. I took whatever job I could find. During the summer months it was always working for a farmer.

Dr. Fath, our school president, took special interest in me and provided me with a number of jobs to take care of my room, tuition, and board. I washed dishes in the college kitchen, rang the bell for change of classes, and for some time fired the boilers to provide heat for the school buildings. He even turned the bookstore over to me to run it as my own since he did not want to be bothered with it. This last job was a real help to me because it kept me in spending money. I soon had a supply of fountain pens, college pendants, freshman skullcaps, monograms for sweaters, as well as other school supplies needed by the students.

To ring the bells for change of classes he had a button installed right above my desk in my room so that I would not have to leave my room during the time I was not attending a class.

The store produced enough revenue so that at the end of the school term I had money left over. My roommate, Edward, often suggested that we go downtown and have a meal in a restaurant for a change. When I mentioned the subject of money, he would say, "Let's go down and borrow it from the bookstore." He knew there was always some change in a cigar box. My friend never failed to pay me back. We were both members of the basketball team, which was one of the best in the conference and won the championship one year.

Edward's parents often sent us a food package containing some good homemade sausage to supplement our diet. These food packages had to be well hidden since there were always food thieves on the lookout. On several occasions we would come into our room and find some grinning neighbor standing in front of the closet with a piece of sausage in his hand.

One of the most unforgettable incidents happened one Sunday afternoon. When most of the students were attending a Christian Endeavor meeting, we decided to go to a nearby pond to spend the afternoon ice-skating. It so happened that I had my skates on first and started to skate across the pond, when I heard Edward yelling, "Paul, come back! The ice is bending under you." The warning had come too late. Just as I was about to turn, thereby causing added weight, the ice broke and I went in to my armpits. Luckily, by breaking the ice ahead of me with my fists, I was able to walk to shore. While standing there kidding my friend about the assistance he had not given me, he suggested that we had better hurry home and change clothes. Running behind me, he kept laughing making all sorts of remarks. "Paul," he said, "do you know that you are beginning to give off steam?" Running, my body generated enough warmth to cause a vapor to come through my clothes.

We got back in time to change and get down to the meeting that had just started. The first song that was announced was "Throw out the life line." I stared at Edward, and he could not resist putting his hand over his mouth and giggling. Not able to control himself, he infected the ones sitting nearby. They, too, joined in the laughter, not knowing why! After the meeting they gathered around and wanted to know what had happened; and, of course, my friend was delighted to tell the whole thing with slight exaggeration.

The following day I would every once in a while hear someone calling to me: "Hey, Paul, when are you going skating again--or is it swimming?"

Once a year the school invited an evangelist to come and hold revival meetings. It was traditional for the ministerial candidates to be converted (born again). Every student was expected to attend, but it was not compulsive. For me these meetings were never too attractive. I quite often baby-sat for married students who had children. I was never quite sure why I disliked these meetings. Possibly it was because of the odor of fire and brimstone that filled the air. It was always impossible for me to identify God with hate and revenge; yet it seemed to be the tactic of the evangelist to scare the converts out of their wits. According to the preacher, the world was run by two deities, God and Satan. Like two zealous politicians, they were competing for supporters. Woe unto him who did not make the right decision-- hell and damnation would be waiting for him. To me that was making God out to be afflicted with all the human frailties. How can God be love and at the same time seek revenge and retribution? Besides, the thought that a mere fly speck in this vast universe should make God angry made no sense.

Evangelists sometimes are so impressed by the power of their rhetoric that they often misrepresent God just to be effective. Instead of glorifying God, they demean Him. When a world-famous evangelist advances the thought that the UFOs are God's angels coming to spy on the earthlings (a sort of CIA), one must consider that nonsense. God does not need tape recorders and bugged telephones to find out what is going one.

The battle between good and evil is waged in man's own heart.

The following are all authentic family photos:

Paul's Parents with son John, Russia around 1893

Paul's father wheat baron Gottlieb Kalmbach II around 1904

who died at age 46

Paul and sisters and brother, Russia around 1905

ИМПЕРАТОРСКОЕ РОССИЙСКОЕ ГЕНЕРАЛЬНОЕ КОНСУЛЬ

въ Берлинѣ.

По указу ЕГО ВЕЛИЧЕСТВА ГОСУДАРЯ ИМПЕРА

**НИКОЛАЯ АЛЕКСАНДРОВИ**

САМОДЕРЖЦА ВСЕРОССІЙСКАГО,

и прочая, и прочая, и прочая.

№ 750

Paul's Papers when he boarded a ship for Canada & USA from Russia at age 16 and escaped the Revolution

Paul's cossack brother John in Russia, around 1910

## МЕТРИЧЕСКАЯ ВЫПИСЬ ИЗЪ СПИСКА РОЖДЕННЫХЪ и КРЕЩЕННЫХЪ

Евангелическо-лютеранскаго Екатеринодарскаго прихода Кубанской об…

Годъ 18__ № ___

| Пол. числ. в. ч. мѣс. рожденія | Пор. день крещенія | Прозвище, имя исключая имя, фамилии и вѣроисповѣданіе родителей; званіе, чинъ, или ремесло отца или матери; или представляющаго мальчика съ крещенію; прозвище проименованія, совершившаго Св. крещеніе и гдѣ оное совершено; имя, фамилія и званіе, тоже имя ремесло воспріемниковъ. | Замѣчанія |
|---|---|---|---|
| 1874<br>Сентября двадцать третьяго дня 23<br>сентября | | № 84<br>Павелъ Отто<br>Родители: Сентавалъ Никендорнъ Беккеръ токаревского цеха<br>съ Мекленбурга ... жена его Анна Марта ур. Лендау/Манда/ лютеранск. исповѣдан. лучъ Тимофеевичъ.<br>Восприемники: Отто Аксельфельдъ Вильгельмовичъ лучъ Тимофеевичъ ... Карлъ Пау Вильгельмовичъ Беккеръ ... 16 сего ноября 1874 г. ... пасторъ | |

№ 444.

Сие удостовѣряется sub fide pastorali съ приложеніемъ ... (М.П.)

> CONSULAT GÉNÉRAL IMPÉRIAL DE RUSSIE
> à Berlin.
>
> Par Ordre de Sa Majesté l'Empereur
> de Toutes les Russies,
> &c. &c. &c.
>
> Le porteur du présent passeport Sujet
> Russe Mr Paul Kalmbach
> âgé de 16 ans
>
> se rend à l'étranger et retourne
> ensuite en Russie.
>
> En foi de quoi et pour lui assurer libre
> passage, je lui ai délivré ce passeport avec apposition
> du sceau du Consulat Général Impérial de Russie.
> Berlin le 29 Août 1913
> N° 750
> (Signé)

E

Paul's 1913 Papers

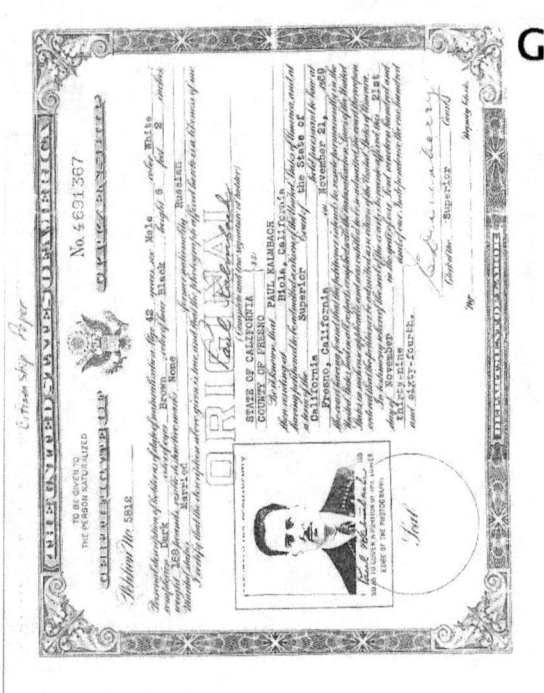

Paul's American Citizenship Papers

Paul after his 1913 arrival in USA and Canada, around 1916

Redfield, South Dakota:
Championship Basketball Team

Paul Changing Tire

Paul's Sisters Mary and Rosalia, in Russia, around 1919

Paul, Redfield College Years

Amelia Ament driving to teach school

Paul's Sisters Mary and Rosalia, in Russia, around 1925

1920s Amelia Ament Kalmbach, the school teacher Paul married

Paul Kalmbach Minister with wife Amelia and daughters, around 1933

Paul's youngest sister Rosalia, 1930s Russia

Paul & Amelia 50s

Paul and his family in America around 1936

Paul taking his youngest daughter to drugstore,
America around 1937

1942    Paul's Daughters

1950s Paul, wife Amelia and their daughters, USA

Paul & Amelia, 60s

Paul's mother Mary Sandau Kalmbach
after sorrow and starvation 40s Russia

1960s Paul's wife Amelia with a favorite family radio

Paul and Amelia 1960s America

An Oil Painting done by Paul with one of his granddaughters, 1971

Around 1966 Paul with some of his grandchildren

1969 Paul with daughter and two of his granddaughters

## Chapter 11
## WORLD WAR I YEARS

WHEN THE UNITED STATES entered the war on the side of England and France to stop the Kaiser, Redfield College had its problems. Since German was spoken on the campus, the hate mongers lost no time in spreading vicious lies against it.

The hysteria was of such intensity that Schumann-Heink's son, who had been a commander in the American navy, said to me, "Even dachshunds were not safe on the streets."

A certain woman living across the street had appointed herself "watchdog" and reported everything that was going on on the campus. One could always see her parting the window curtains to peek.

One day the college had barrels of sweeping compound unloaded and stored in the basement of the administration building. Our detective across the street lost no time in reporting to the city authorities that the college was storing ammunition and guns. Needless to say, the investigators left quite red-faced after having broken into barrels and having found nothing but treated sawdust. These hateful people never once tried to find out how many college students had left school for the trenches, to face the German army. They could only see students who happened to keep step as they walked through town.

The college glee club was invited to participate in a war bond rally held in one of the theaters. One director had the choir sing "The Soldiers' Chorus." That was an affront that our lady spy could not tolerate, and she set to work writing a venomous article for the local paper, stating: "These Huns had the audacity to sing a German victory song at an American rally!" The woman was just too ignorant to realize that music is a universal language and does not belong to one people.

Some of our "college Huns" soon thereafter themselves were shooting at their brothers. But we had to be careful not to keep step when appearing in town. The people of the city were good and reasonable people. The situation simply demonstrated what one hateful person could accomplish.

At this time I still had hope of one day returning home to Russia, and had as yet made no attempt to become a citizen. After Russia had pulled out of the conflict, there was still continuous fighting going on between the Bolsheviks and the White Russians. After 1918 Russia began to face a food shortage. The fighting was particularly fierce in the Black Sea area and the Caucasus. My home village changed hands between the opposing forces twice in one day.

For a long period of time all correspondence was suspended, and I had no idea of what was going on. My people were residing in the fighting zone. Would they still be alive? Again the restlessness and the nightmares set in, but I forced myself to keep going. So I went back to washing dishes, to shoveling coal, to ringing bells and selling fountain pens, and back to my books.

Dr. Fath called me to his office to give me some words of comfort. He stressed the fact that a nervous breakdown would help no one, least of all my mother--if she was still alive. As always, he made good sense and helped me to keep a proper perspective. But at the end of the school year he said to me, "I was never so glad to have a school year end. I was afraid that some of us were beginning to break under the load."

At last the war had come to an end. The armistice was signed, and the killing and maiming stopped. The nation had reason to break out in hysterical joy. There was dancing in the streets. Everybody was happy and *belonged*. Hatred had given way to friendship and kindness. Complete sanity and tolerance had returned. The students could again walk the streets unmolested. Some of the students serving in the armed forces returned home and came back to the college. We were again considered good Americans--a fact which should never have been doubted in the first place.

At last a letter from home. This time a letter from sister Rosalia. She had married an electrical engineer, the son of my former schoolteacher. They lived in Sochi by the Black Sea. Sochi was considered the Riviera of Russia.

She brought me details of what had happened. Brother John had finally married. His bride had come from a prominent Jewish family by the name of Zelensky. He was still connected with the Rostov Bank.

What a miraculous effect her letter had upon me! It made me feel as if I had gone through a health spa. Always in love with life, I had received new vitality and again was my mischievous self. I had guarded my sorrow as if it were a secret trust to be shared with no one. Now the sun was again shining.

With my mind temporarily at ease, things were again happening in the dormitory.

One of the professors had the room across the hall from mine. He was somewhat of an eccentric and quite often the butt of a joke. It was again the two immigrants, Fred and

Paul, who collaborated in doing mischief.

It was a Sunday night. The dormitory was practically empty. Everybody was either attending church or out on a date. My friend and I hit upon the idea to put a stuffed dummy into the professor's bed. Getting hold of an old union suit, we stuffed it with old rags; we also adjusted a half a pitcher of water inside the dummy. It was tilted in such a way that lifting the dummy the least bit would spill the water and wet the bed.

Lights out, we were waiting in my room for the old professor to come home. About midnight we heard him entering his room. We listened. We heard some angry growling, then the noise of a window being raised. There was no doubt that the intruder would be evicted via the open window. The force with which he grabbed the dummy naturally caused the dummy to do the unforgivable--namely to wet the bed. The professor had to sleep that night on the floor.

The next morning a nonresident student,

coming to attend classes, saw a hilarious sight. Outside the professor's window, straddled grotesquely across the power line, was a dummy. It could not help but attract attention. Students walked into their classrooms with smiles on their faces. Those entering the professor's room asked him what had happened to his roommate. It was the talk of the day.

Since I was the closest neighbor, it was only natural that he should ask me whether I knew something about it and who had been behind the prank. I was still a poor hand at confessing and pleaded innocence. However, for a few days thereafter I had the eerie feeling that a pair of eyes were following me around whenever the professor was nearby. My co-worker kept his lips sealed, and the professor was never able to point the finger.

Halloween was always a good time for extracurricular activity. I thought that a little prank on my friend and benefactor, Dr. Fath, would do no harm. There was a big rock on his lawn. It was hard work, but I managed to roll it onto his porch.

The next day President Fath called me to his office. When I entered he looked over his glasses and said to me, "Paul, some smart aleck had a good time dumping a heavy rock on my porch. Will you be good enough to remove it?" "Sure thing. Be glad to," I answered. Leaving his office, I could not help stealing a glance in his direction. He had returned to his paperwork and was pretending to be quite busy. He could have gotten away with his act of innocence had he only kept his fat stomach from vibrating. His face was sober enough, but the rest of his torso was laughing.

I was sure no one had witnessed the heavy work I had done the night before. So how did he know? Oh, well, well-known astronnomer that he was, he may have seen it in the stars. Anyway, he was a good sport. I thought the world of that man.

## Chapter 12
## THEOLOGY

STARTING A COURSE in theology had a sobering effect upon me. I forced myself to become more serious and conduct myself with the decorum befitting a student of theology.

The bookstore gave me an opportunity to page through book catalogues and acquire a few books that particularly fascinated me and aroused my curiosity; books like *The Riddle of the Universe*, by Haeckel, *Thus Spake Zarathustra*, by Nietzsche; *The Mistakes of Moses*, by Ingersoll; and *The Philosophy of Spinoza*.

These books were hardly conducive to building a solid foundation in conservative theology, especially for a beginner. Subsequently I began to use up a lot of time in class asking questions. One of the first questions that bothered me was related to the Creation. "When God supposedly spoke the first four words, 'Let there be light,' " I asked, "what language did God use?" I could not resist interrupting the professor while he was giving his lectures. It irritated him to such an extent that he once suggested I choose another profession and not try to become a minister.

This was something that I could not understand. Why should not the teaching of the church rest upon a foundation so solid that nothing could shake it? Even Jesus permitted a doubting disciple to touch the scars in this hands and side, left by the crucifixion, in order to convince Thomas so there would never be any doubt when in the future he would speak of the resurrection of his Master. The truth! I wanted to be sure that whatever I wanted other people to believe I would also believe.

One day after one of those controversial hours, the professor came to my dormitory room to have a private discussion with me. When I let him in, he went straight to my bookcase to look at what I had on the shelves. Reading the titles out loud, he kept nodding his head, saying, "No wonder you are so full of questions. All those books you are reading are poison! You should not read these books!"

I did not dare to ask him how he knew they were poison if he had not read them, but managed to answer, "Even if these books are of a controversial nature, should not the Christian teaching be a strong enough antidote for any kind of poison? Were not the men who brought about the Reformation skeptics? Only by getting the questions that bother me properly and satisfactorily answered can I hope to build a foundation that will hold together once I am out trying to preach to others." Again he cut me short.

"I think you would do much better in some other profession," he said and left. This, however, was not the end of it. It was becoming clearer every day that we had less and less respect for each other. I was beginning to be a thorn in his side, and he, to me, seemed intellectually dishonest.

One day, as he was lecturing on sin and the remission of sin, he spoke of Jesus' hanging on the cross and in his dying moment forgiving a sinner who had been crucified with him. I held up my hand, interrupting him to pose a question. He gave me permission to speak. Presenting my problem in the form of a corollary, I went on: "Suppose a man lived his entire life by doing good, having dedicated himself to serving God. Maybe sacrificing his life in a heathen mission field. Suddenly one disaster after the other falls on him and his family. He loses his wife, his children, everything. He stands there alone and heartbroken and queries, 'How could God permit this misfortune to happen to one who served him so faithfully?' In that moment of great despair he finds himself doubting God, even as did Jesus when he called out, 'My God, my God, why hast thou forsaken me?' Mind you, though, the doubt was only of temporary nature. But at that very moment he drops dead, presumably an atheist. Will he be forever condemned? Now, I cannot believe that God would ignore all the good that a man has done during his lifetime while at the same time admitting a thief and murderer into paradise just because he died a believer. Would that not mean that under certain conditions God rewards the evildoer and punishes the righteous? That I just cannot believe. It most certainly would contradict the fact that God is love."

I was beginning to wonder whether the wonderful teachings of the Nazarene had not been dogmatize and denominationalized beyond recognition. Would I find the answers to my doubts, or would I eventually have to take the professor's advice and get into some other kind of work besides the ministry? Doubts, doubts, and more doubts began to descend upon me like vampire bats thirsting for the lifeblood of my faith.

Fortunately, one of the faculty members, a countryman of mine who also had come to America as a young man, had a more liberal outlook on life and did not condemn me for my seeming agnosticism but rather encouraged it. To him, a student who asked questions was a student who did some thinking. That man was not only a competent teacher who had thoroughly mastered his subjects, but also a friend. Through him came my conviction that every individual has to be the architect of his faith. There can be diversification in the form and façade of our spiritual dwellings, just as there is in our earthly dwellings. Though different in style and size, all have one thing in common: they give us warmth in the wintertime and protection against heat in the summertime. As long as one believes in God, who is love, the name of the church or denomination is secondary.

After my second year in the seminary, the time came for me to try my wings. The ministers serving on the school board were helpful in placing the students during the three summer months in rural churches. It gave them an opportunity to practice preaching and gain experience in ministerial work.

The Reverend Strauch, serving a parish in Sterling, Colorado, arranged for me to serve in a small country church near Proctor,

Colorado. At least ninety percent of the members of this church were closely related. The old patriarch was still quite active and could be seen making his daily rounds, visiting his six sons and his daughter. They were all good-sized families. Grandpa's last stopping place was always the home where the minister stayed. He was very familiar with life in Russia and enjoyed spinning tales. In relating some of his nostalgia he sometimes got carried away exaggerating and read the reaction in my face. His delightful sense of humor would cause him to interrupt his narrative with giggles and say, "The pastor does not believe everything I say." I had the feeling that he sometimes deliberately stretched the truth in order to test me. I often regretted in later life that he did not live long enough to see this young minister, with whom he had swapped so many stories, become his grandson.

Room and board for the first month was furnished by the Kriegers. Mrs. Krieger was the baby sister in the Ament clan. They had three children: Arthur, Ruby and baby

Polly. They also had the grandparents, the Kriegers, staying with them. It had always been my good fortune to attract little children. As a matter of fact, they have always been my best instructors in theology. In them I could see the image that adults should have. Little Polly became so attached to me that whenever her mother was trying to get her ready for bed, the little one would clutch her dress and say, "No--peach shoul (preacher should)." She insisted that getting her ready for bed was the preacher's job. It was the same every night, and none enjoyed the play more than the grandparents. It had become part of my ministerial services to put little Polly to bed, a service that I enjoyed immensely.

During the church service on Sunday, Polly would manage to get away from her mother and come right behind the pulpit and sit in my chair. Since the congregation was just one big happy family, no one minded the distraction, least of all the minister. The devotion and innocence displayed by that little child was a far better sermon than

I could have preached anyway.

After the first month, I was passed on to the home of Conrad Ament, who was the second oldest in the family. My stay with this wonderful family was sheer delight. Conrad was a very kindly, quiet man. His wife, "Aunt Alice," was very jolly and outgoing. She was the best cook. Her chicken noodle soup was unsurpassed.

The two teenaged sons and two teenaged girls kept things lively. The boys were direct opposites in nature. Jacob, the older, was quiet and easygoing and had a tremendous sense of humor. David was the one always monopolizing the conversation. Any subject that David brought up always brought forth some humorous interjection from Jacob. They were like a couple of comedians, one of them acting as the straight man. David made the mistake once, while at the dinner table, of remarking that he, too, would like to study for the ministry. From that moment on, Jacob always referred to his brother as "the pastor." It was always "Pass the butter, pastor" or

"Pass the bread, pastor." The mother would shake with laughter, and the father would just smile and shake his head. The youngest in the family, twelve-year-old Lydia, was a tomboy. After she discovered that I was corresponding with a young lady, she enjoyed racing me to the mailbox to get the letters. It was almost a daily event.

It was a wonderful summer for me. The joy I discovered in ministering to people who responded so wonderfully to my efforts was for me much needed therapy. I found that I was able to bring to people a message of worth despite my many theological uncertainties and doubts. That intimate contact with people helped to encourage me to keep on the track.

Back in school, I was contacted one day by the traveling secretary, John Reister, whose job it was to raise money for the support of the school. He had returned from Canada and brought me the news that he had discovered a family in Irvine, Alberta, Canada, by the name of Samuel Kalmbach, who claimed close kinship with me and begged that I come and stay with them the next summer. I could help out in the store, clerking, and so forth, and would be reimbursed for my service. I was glad to accept the invitation and looked forward to it.

Arriving in Irvine, I had no difficulty spotting Sam on the station platform. He had the same build as grandfather Kalmbach, and looked more like him than my own father did. I walked right up to him. It made him very happy to think that even though I had never seen him before, I was able to recognize the Kalmbach stature and build. He took me to his home and introduced me to his wife and four daughters.

The oldest was eighteen years old, and the youngest was ten years old. They all seemed happy to have at last found a relative bearing the same name.

The fact that my father's name was the same as grandfather's had Samuel making the mistake of thinking that it was my father who was his uncle, when in fact it was my grandfather who was the brother to his father, Christian Kalmbach. But it did not matter. We had come from the same clan.

Clerking in the store was a new and fascinating experience for me. Always interested in people, I found this to be a great opportunity to study the different customers. For instance, there was an old widower who came to the store almost every day. One could always see him standing in front of the egg basket with an egg in each hand, weighing and balancing them as if his hands were scales. He was sure to get his money's worth. He was a frugal old man, and no one ever bothered him.

There were two characters who had uncanny timing and always appeared in the store at the same time--as if prearranged. They had both served in the Russian army and together had taken part in the Russo-Japanese war. They would always start an argument, accusing each other of having lost the war. One would start by saying, "It was all your fault! You and General

Kuropatkin made Russia lose the war!" The other one then would counter, "Well, I was not in the battle of Mugden when the Russians were defeated, but you were. How come you did not stand fast and challenge the Japs instead of trying to outrun everyone for cover?" The first one answered, "If you had had a bunch of Japs aiming at your behind, you would have run for cover, too." So on and on went the argument, to the delight of other customers. They knew they were putting on a show and enjoyed it.

The summer went by fast, and I was glad I had come to spend the summer with relatives. However, during my stay I did notice Samuel lapsing into quiet and sad moods. He took many trips out to his cattle ranch just to get away from the business and generally showed that he was worried. The collection tours he made, trying to get some of his customers to pay their bills, were not profitable. The people had had several crop failures in succession and just had no money. Any business can carry just so much on their books, and one cannot restock the business with book credit.

I had been back in school for only a very short time when I received a telegram from the oldest daughter, Edith, that upset me very much: "Papa died of a heart attack. Can you come?" I had known that lovely family only a little while, but in that time I had fallen in love with them all--they had actually become my family. Not a stranger to grief, I was very sympathetic and knew exactly how that family felt. Sam was about the same age as my father had been when he passed away. There were four children orphaned; there had been four orphans left in my family. There was so much similarity in every way that I felt I was reliving some of my own past. Thinking back how the family was depending upon my brother John to take care of the family, I felt that the family was calling for an older brother to come and at least help out for a time. It presented a problem for me. Should I follow reason and stay in school to finish my last year or answer the call for help? I was again the boy in Russia who thought he had to buy a present for each member of the family. Ignoring the call would have left me with a feeling of guilt. I had to go, even though it meant graduating one year later.

The school authorities could not see it my way and tried to change my mind, but I had to follow my conscience. To my surprise, the professor who had once made the suggestion that perhaps it would be best if I chose a different profession was now the most vehement in stressing the importance of staying and finishing the course. Evidently he had come to the conviction that the young agnostic was not entirely hopeless. But my mind had been made up. Nothing and no one would be able to change it. As it turned out, it was a serious mistake, and I often regretted it.

There was not much I could do except give some moral support to the bereaved family. As far as the business was concerned, it was a repetition of our own history with the mill. Sam had become a wealthy man, and his creditors had faith in him that somehow he would overcome all difficulties and again become solvent. But with Sam out of the picture, these creditors became nervous and began to demand payments on their accounts. Since the last two years' business was all on the books and no money had come in, satisfying the creditors was impossible.

The credit company made me the manager of the store. It soon became obvious that they realized the hopelessness of the situation and would try to get rid of the store at any price.

The company confronted me with the proposition that if I could come up with at least one thousand dollars they would sell the store to me and carry the mortgage for the balance. They no doubt figured that at least that much money would give them a few months, and after that the outcome would be the same--they would have one thousand dollars and the store, too.

All the money I had to my name was two hundred and fifty dollars. Mulling the proposition over in my mind, I had certain apprehensions about trying to effect that kind of solution. For one thing, how would it look to the family, no matter how hopeless the whole situation was? As far as the family was concerned, the business was lost. But my owning it, no matter under what conditions, would look suspicious. I wanted to help, not hurt, the family.

I called up a good friend of mine to discuss the offer with him and what would be required to swing the deal. George Wolff offered to go into partnership with me and come up with the asked-for down payment. Together we took a trip to Calgary to negotiate. The deal was made, and we bought the store for forty cents on the dollar. The general merchandise business now would be Wolff and Kalmbach.

Neither Wolff not I had any delusions about the success of the business. We knew that it would depend entirely on the next wheat crop. If there was any crop at all, we would be able to make it; but if another crop failure was imminent, then we would be up against it.

After returning from Calgary, we kept the store closed for several days. We even had paper over the windowpanes so that no one would be able to look in to see what was going on. During that time we tagged every item, getting ready for a gigantic sale.

The day of the opening was a huge success. People were standing on the sidewalk to get in. We did not know where the money suddenly came from. We took in enough on the first day to make an additional payment to the credit company. People were talking of the new firm that had come to life. Wolff and I, however, knew that this initial success meant nothing if there were no wheat harvest. Like Samuel before us, we still had to sell mostly on credit. True, the people had hidden a few dollars for emergencies such as the sale, but that was all.

Summer came along, and the sky stayed cloudless. The fields were drying up-- another drought was in sight. The fields presented a heartbreaking sight. Some of the farmers did not even bother to take their machines out of the sheds. I was convinced that there certainly would be no future for me unless I went back to school.

I offered to sell my partnership to George for five hundred dollars. He agreed to give me two hundred and fifty dollars in cash and a promissory note for the rest. I got ready to go back to school but not back to the seminary. Still unconvinced that the ministry was actually what I wanted, I decided on a detour and went to Chicago instead. My decision was inspired by an attorney friend in whose presence I had offered certain opinions regarding a criminal case that was reported in the newspaper. The attorney thought that I would make a criminal lawyer and really should strongly consider going to school with that in mind. He even offered to support me--provided I promised to join his firm. Well, it may have been an offer in jest, but it helped me to decide on taking up the study of law. My destination was set for Chicago.

## Chapter 13
### CHICAGO AND DESTINY

CHICAGO PROVED TO BE MY city of destiny. It made me feel almost like a newly arrived immigrant again. It most assuredly would have some effect upon my life. Here I was in my mid-twenties changing course to become a criminal lawyer instead of going into the ministry. Instead of saving sinners, as it were, I was to become a defender of sinners.

When brother John learned of my decision, he was elated and commented, "I am glad that you have finally come to your senses!" He had never shown any enthusiasm over the fact that his younger brother was destined to become a minister. True, I remembered his attending church every Sunday to please mother, but he would most of the time come into the church auditorium just before the pastor pronounced the benediction. He always explained that the benediction was all he wanted.

The news of my detour, however, had a different effect upon mother. She was sure that I had come under a bad influence, and prayed that I might eventually return to my original goal. Her letter indicated that she had a strong feeling that something was wrong; and her intuition, as always, was quite right. But again, as when I had gambled her marketing money away, she did not reprimand me but closed with the following: "Naturally I am disappointed that you have chosen to become a lawyer instead of a minister, but as long as you did not feel called upon to devote your life to the service of God, it would have been wrong for you to enter the ministry."

Mother had not forgotten how to attack my weaker side. Very cleverly she included the sentence, "You have chosen not to serve the Lord." Of course, that was a slight distortion of the truth, but there was a purpose behind it which eventually would be a factor.

I rented a room on Jackson Boulevard,

near Cicero. My landlady was a doctor's widow. She had three other tenants. The atmosphere in her home was congenial. She was very pleased by the fact that I worshiped my mother and thought so much of my family, and she took it upon herself to keep checking up on me to see whether I had forgotten to write to my mother.

Chicago was also the home of the Congregational superintendent, Dr. Obenhaus. His younger son and I had become good friends and for a time attended a night course that was part of the LaSalle Extension University. But Dr. Obenhaus never failed to urge me to return to the ministry. As yet I was not to be dissuaded from pressing toward my new chosen goal.

An early crisis had presented itself, again causing a temporary change of plans. I had very much depended on the rest of the money that Wolff owed me, but I received a letter from him informing me that he was unable to pay me the money and that I would have to forfeit it. He claimed that his business had failed and it would be no more than fair that I should be willing to lose with him. I wrote back and told him that I believed him and told him to forget about the note. Having worked on Saturdays in a certain ladies' shoe store, I was offered a steady job. But I could not see myself selling shoes the rest of my life so I went job hunting. The employment agency sent me to be interviewed by the manager of the Liggett and Myer Tobacco Company. I was accepted in the advertising department and was given a covered Ford car that looked like a miniature van with advertising painted all over it. The territory that was assigned to me was South Chicago. The first day out I felt rather foolish and a bit ashamed to think that I, a former candidate for the ministry, was on my way to peddle pipe tobacco. But since my manager, who went along with me to introduce me to the territory, was an elderly Methodist deacon, I was somewhat comforted.

The storekeepers in the territory were

primarily Italian and Jewish. I got along with them very well, especially the Jews. Some of them even invited me for Sunday dinners. We had much in common because they, too, had come from Russia. The fact that I had Jewish relatives also helped. They even kept insisting that I was Jewish, despite my denial. "You are as much a Jew as I am," one would say. "Why deny it? It's written all over you!"

Anyway, my boss got wind of it, that I was getting along so well, and made quite a to-do about it in sales meetings, stressing the fact that if a green newcomer could get along so well with his customers, and especially Jews, the other salesmen would do well to follow the example.

I did not appreciate being held up as an example; it was hardly conducive to making friends out of the rest of the salesmen. I got up to explain that it was not superior salesmanship that accounted for my apparent success among the Jewish storekeepers but the fact that we considered ourselves former countrymen, all coming from Europe.

The office manager had to take a trip to Gary, Indiana, and called on me to furnish the transportation. Since he was an active churchworker we traded various experiences we both had had in that field. The conversation drifted into a discussion of the various ethnic groups and districts in Chicago. He indicated that since my district was predominantly Italian and the main hangout for the South Chicago beer baron, Dean O'Banion, I should be very cautious.

It was not long before I had my first shocking experience. One morning, arriving in my district, I parked my car, took my sample case, and started down the street. For some unexplainable reason I stopped in the middle of the block and decided to jaywalk and cross over to the other side of the street. I knew it was against the law; yet the urge was irresistible. Just as I set foot on the sidewalk on the opposite side of the street, I heard a gunshot coming from the very corner where I would have been had I kept on down the street and not crossed in the middle. People were seen running over to the spot, and naturally I ran down also to see what had happened. A tenant had shot his landlord through the head. The man was lying in a pool of blood. He was making jerky reflex motions as if he were trying to get away. His head lay motionless, but his legs thrashed in the blood. It was a shocking scene. Uniformed policemen soon appeared on the scene, asking questions. No one had any information. There seemed to have been not one single witness to the shooting. It was as if they were all trained to keep quiet and not get involved.

Seeing that man's twitching body lying in a pool of blood was so upsetting to me that I had to discontinue my route that day and drive home. There was always something going on in that district. Seeing a well-dressed man in a blue serge suit and white socks walking in and out of stores, I asked the storekeeper the man's identity. The merchant was surprised that I did not know and answered, "That man is Dean

O'Banion."

This man was later killed by his rivals. One just could not avoid coming in contact with violators of the prohibition law.

One Sunday morning the salesmen staying at the same house with me had a visitor. He was driving a new Buick sedan and offered to take us all for a ride. I was glad to go along. It was soon obvious that our host knew how to handle the wheel. He darted in and out of traffic as if the car were part of his body. We wound up in North Chicago in a garage that had several floors of parking space above it. After reaching the very top, we drove into an area filled with trucks neatly parked in line and covered with canvas. They were obviously ready to roll. My curiosity made me ask the driver what these trucks were carrying. He nonchalantly answered, "Beer, and the truck next to the door is mine."

Pretending to be calm, I was nevertheless shocked. He also told us that his boss was Bugs Moran, another beer baron, active in the district. This garage was the same place where later the St. Valentine's Day massacre took place. I was thinking on our way home that all I needed now was to take a trip to Cicero and meet some of Al Capone's boys. I was glad to get back to my room.

As a tobacco salesman, I knew that sooner or later I would come to another forked road and would have to make a definite decision about my future. I certainly could not be a tobacco salesman the rest of my life. That fork came sooner than I had expected, through an event that I could not help but consider a miracle.

There was a certain store in the neighborhood owned by a crippled old lady. My boss had warned me and said that the best thing to do was to stay out of that store. "That woman," he said, "hobbling around on crutches is a veritable dragon. She is rude and insulting and does not like salespeople." On that particular day I felt tempted to enter the store in order to see the lady with that terrible reputation. She could do no more than chase me out, I thought. I went in. The bell suspended above the door announced my entrance. She came hobbling in through the back door and glared at me. "What do you want?" she asked. I tipped my hat and stated my mission. She pointed towards the door and merely said, "Out!" Amused, I bowed, tipped my hat again, thanked her for the reception, and left.

As I made my way around the block, I noticed that the block was a triangle. It gave me an idea. I went into the same store again. "Are you back again!" she barked. I smiled and apologized, blaming the fact that the block had only three sides. At that she laughed.

I prolonged my apology as long as I could, in the meantime opening my sample case and switching right over into my sales pitch. To my surprise, she listened. I was beginning to sense a victory that really would surprise my boss. Reaching for my order pad, I had another surprise. She reached out and lightly touched my hand to stop me from going any further. She said,

"Young man, I don't need a thing. I just liked listening to you. You should not be wasting your time peddling tobacco. You should be behind a pulpit, preaching."

Stunned, I stood there facing her, my chin slightly sagging. Finally closing the sample case, I muttered, "Lady, that is exactly what I am going to do." Before leaving the store, I took time to explain to her what a wonderful thing she had accomplished by turning my path in the right direction. Her face became radiant with happiness. It was the kind of joy that manifests itself when realizing that one has been of real service to someone else. She wished me luck and hoped that she would be able sometime to hear me preach.

Leaving the store, I was overcome with emotion.. In that crippling woman I had seen my mother. Losing no time, I called Dr. Obenhaus and asked him whether he had a church for me. He was simply delighted and said that he just happened to have the right spot for me, a small church subsidized by the Home Mission and located in the college town of York, Nebraska. Not only would I be serving a church but completing my college education as well.

When I told my boss on the following morning that I had decided to go back and continue school, he said to me, "Paul, you have a promising future with this company, and I can promise you that before too long you would have a subdivision. But since I know the reason you are leaving us, I can only wish you good luck. If you ever feel like coming back, we'll have an opening for you."

Of course, I had no other choice but to take the direction that crippled old lady had pointed out to me. It was more than shallow advice; it was a miracle brought about by my mother's prayers. The angel on my shoulder was still with me.

## Chapter 14
# BACK TO CHURCH AND COLLEGE

YORK, NEBRASKA, WAS A CLEAN and orderly college town inhabited by middle-class people. The college was subsidized by the United Brethren Church and was a well-run institution.

The town was also known for its strong KKK organization. It was here that I saw for the first time the spectacle of a burning cross and hooded Klansmen staging a parade through town.

On the campus I was considered a foreign student. There was all kinds of rumors floating around--some quite flattering. For instance, it was held that I was a member of the upper class and had escaped to avoid falling in the hands of the Bolsheviks. Others had a suspicion that I might be a Russian spy. Even the college president called me to his office for an interrogation as to my political stand. He did not want a Communist on his campus. Luckily I succeeded in satisfying him that I was neither a spy nor a Communist.

The church I was serving had about a hundred members, mostly second-generation German-Russians. Carrying a full college course and taking care of the church kept me quite busy. Again I found that preaching and serving in my small capacity made me feel happy. There simply is magic in serving people.

Dr. Obenhaus had mentioned to me that York College had a well-known professor of psychology and a very competent instructor. He was also the dean of the school. I was privileged to have most of my classes under him. He occasionally gave practical demonstrations in hypnotism, which were always enjoyed by the class. In connection with my psychology study I was reading a book called *The Psychic Health of Jesus.* In a private discussion with the professor, I mentioned the book to him, and some of the facts brought out by various psychologists. He asked me whether he could have the book for a few days, and I was glad to lend it to him.

After a few days he asked me one day to remain after class. He wanted to discuss my book with me.

In his opinion the book had definite merits but since it dealt with psychoanalyzing Jesus, he felt it should not be circulated among the students. It was a conservative school and psychoanalyzing Jesus would be frowned upon. So even this brilliant mind was afraid of anything contradicting tradition and church creeds. But he was a man who could listen to one's problems with sympathy and understanding. I had great respect for him.

While discussing bigotry and intolerance, the question of the KKK came up. The professor wanted to know my attitude in the matter. My answer was that I thought the KKK was an anachronism in a democratic society and should not be tolerated. There should be no discrimination, no classifying people as those who are 100 percent American and those who are less than 100 percent American. The immigrant who comes to this country and applies for citizenship makes a great sacrifice by severing relations with his native land. Not only that, but he takes a special oath of allegiance to his adopted country so that there will be no doubt as to his loyalty. He should not be told by someone parading in disguise that he is a class B citizen. Most of these people burning crosses and staging parades, boasting about what great patriots they are, inherited their citizenship. They have done nothing to earn it. A wealth that has been acquired through sweat and tears has certainly as much value as, if not more than, inherited wealth.

The dean agreed that the argument was valid and himself expressed similar sentiments.

One of my younger church members was very boastful about the fact that he was a Klansman. I asked him whether he thought that he was a better citizen than his naturalized father. He could only shrug his shoulders.

My student life in York was pleasant. I lived only two blocks from the school campus and was able to take advantage of the tennis courts. The athletic coach came to me one day with an old newspaper clipping describing a basketball game, mentioning my name. He asked me whether I had been a member of that team. When I answered in the affirmative, he said to me, "Why in the hell are you not on my team?" He persuaded me to join the team and also turn out for football.

My football career was of short duration. When I appeared on a Sunday morning behind the pulpit sporting a black eye and a blue nose bridge, some of my members thought it was a bit too distracting. So I quit.

As for basketball, the first game we played against a visiting team, I was put in the lineup but found that I was not wanted. No one would pass me the ball even though I stood free under the basket. That marked the end of basketball for me.

At last I received a letter from brother

John. He wrote and told me that if I could get him a visa, he, too, would come to America. The Soviet government had made him the promise that if he could get a visa, they would permit him to leave the country if he left his wife and child behind. The presumption, no doubt, was that as long as the wife and son could be held as hostages, he would do nothing to discredit Communism abroad. The prospect of soon seeing my brother made me delirious with joy.

It so happened that one of my classmates was a U.S. senator's daughter. We were good friends, and when I told her my problem she offered to help by getting me an appointment with her father. The senator was very gracious and obliging. In a short time a visa was in my hands. At last I could do something for my brother.

The euphoria was destined to be of short duration. He received the visa, but when he informed the Soviet government that he had it, they demanded in addition an enormous sum of money that he was certain to be unable to raise. In short, they did not want him to leave. His job in the bank was taken away from him, and he had to fend for himself. He was fortunate that one of his hobbies came in to save the situation and permit him to earn a living for his family. He went into photography.

The ordeal made him quite despondent and caused him to brood. Mother was frightened. She sent me a letter in which she expressed the fear that the situation could possibly drive him to suicide, and she asked me to write him.

My problem was what to say to someone whom I admired and had taken as an example all my life. It was always he who had given *me* advice. Mother also mentioned that she was overjoyed to learn that I had again returned to the ministry. She was convinced that it was an answer to her prayers. When John noticed her crying for joy, he was supposed to have said to her, "You finally got your wish. Why are you crying now?" But tears do not come through remorse only, but also through extreme happiness.

I decided to do as mother wanted me to do and write to brother. It was not only a letter from one brother to another, but it was also a pastor stretching out a hand to one who needed it.

> My dear brother,
> Just received a letter from our dear mother. She poured her heart out to me and revealed some facts concerning you that made me feel very, very sad. My other brother! Do you remember our parting at Bremerhaven? You were walking along the dock, trying to keep pace with the ship that was taking me away. You kept waving your hat, and I waved back. We continued as long as we were able to see each other. As long as I was able to see you I was able to control myself. When finally you disappeared from

sight and I saw nothing but sky and water, I broke down and wept. These tears were different from tears you had seen so often in the past. These were tears that had suddenly come from a man. I realized that the turbulence and tossing of the ship by the strong ocean waves was symbolic of what my life from then on would be. The pilot wheel would be in my own hands. Dear brother, my tears this time were the result of a painful rebirth that had taken place. I had broken out of the cocoon of my protected childhood and youth and had emerged from the metamorphosis a *man*! I suddenly sensed an inner strength and was prepared for whatever the future would bring. Behind this newfound strength

was something that had
brought it about. It had
not originated with me,
but had come from anoth-
er source--namely, our
dear mother.

Through the years I have
always felt her hand on my
shoulder, encouraging me to
keep going. My other source
of strength was a young man
with whom I had spent the
first fifteen years of my life
--my dear brother.

When father died, you
stepped into father's shoes
and shouldered his respon-
sibilities like a man. You
were and still remain my
idol. I shall always try to
emulate you.

John, I would like to put
my hand on your shoulder as
your younger brother, look
you in the eye, and say to you:

Brother, you taught me how to fight. Now stay my example! You are older than I, no doubt wiser in many ways, but from my own painful experience, let me confess that I was in the greatest danger when I came close to atheism. When I tried to follow the advice of Nietzche, Schopenhauer, and Haeckel. How much easier my burdens became when I turned for help to Him who said, "Come unto me, you who are heavy laden, and I will give you rest."

   Brother, you have a wife and son. Look into their faces, and you will get the courage to carry on. The air you breathe, the food you eat, will always be the same. The strength that is within you determines

whether you are a free
man. Let nothing defeat
you!
                Your devoted and
                loving brother.

  The answer to the letter that I received showed that I had struck a responsive chord, and he thanked me most heartily. For the first time he said, "I hope that the ministry will always keep you in that happy and contented frame of mind." It was the last time that I ever heard from him directly.

## Chapter 15
## MY FIRST PARISH

AFTER YORK COLLEGE, Dr. Obenhaus suggested that I accept a call from a newly organized church in Cheyenne, Wyoming. The parish consisted of two churches. The country church near Grover, Colorado, had to be served every third Sunday.

The Cheyenne people were mostly railroad employees and middle-aged. There were hardly any children above the age of eleven years.

On Saturdays I held school in the church building. The parishioners were anxious for their children to receive instruction in the German language as well as Bible history and the tenets of the religion. This was the part of the ministry that gave me the greatest pleasure.

The short time I served this church was not without some amusing incidents. The fact that I was rooming in a bachelors' apartment house downtown did not sit

very well with some of the people.
They were always afraid that their young
minister might fall into bad company and
were quite disturbed about it.

Someone got the bright idea to test, or,
rather, tempt, the minister and thus find out
whether he could be trusted to be left in the
aforementioned surroundings.

One evening, quite late, I was already
preparing to retire when there was a knock
at my door. Slipping into my bathrobe, I
answered the door. To my great surprise
there stood a young and attractive widow.
Since we had a Negro doorman whose
partial duty was to keep women out of the
building, it was a mystery to me how she
had been able to gain access. It was
obvious to me that she expected to be
invited in. However, leaning on one side
of the door, I barred the entrance by putting
my arms across it, bracing myself on the
other side. She kept stretching her neck,
trying to peek into my room. The gesture
was unmistakable. But I stood like Horatio
at the bridge. She was not to pass! Asking

her to what I owed the honor of having such a late and charming visitor, she replied that she had come to find our whether she could send her six-year-old boy to my Saturday school. Giving her the benefit of the doubt, I thought that perhaps she had not been attending the service when I announced from the pulpit that all children of six years and older would be welcome to attend. She apologized and by this time was noticeably blushing. She realized that I suspected something.

After she left, I mulled over the whole incident and became convinced that this young woman, who usually sat far enough to the front so the minister could see the generous contribution she always dropped into the collection plate, was acting out a definite plan. The answer was not long in coming.

Several days later I was walking across the viaduct on my way to the church when I heard a man calling from below and motioning me to wait for him. It was a section foreman who with his crew was doing some repair work on the railroad tracks. He was also one of my deacons.

He grabbed my hand and started to "pump" it while saying with a big grin on his face, "Congratulations, Reverend. I am proud of you. You are OK."

I said, "But I don't why I am being congratulated."

"Well, first, before I explain, I want to apologize, having been a party to a conspiracy that could have had embarrassing results. You see, I was in the widow's store the other day, and she and I got to talking about your bachelor apartment. She offered to make a wager that she could get into your apartment. I accepted the bet. Yesterday, when I came into her store to check on the results, she would not even talk to me. I knew then that she had failed, and she admitted it. So while I am again apologizing, I also repeat, I am proud of you."

Jokingly, I responded, "Well I had to live up to the rules of the house, don't you know!"

We both laughed and parted. Then he called after me, "Reverend, I don't think that King David could have resisted!"

I strode on to my little church building with my shining armor undamaged and untarnished. I realized, however, that sometime soon I would have to give romance some attention and find a mate.

There were many matchmakers offering to help. The most persistent of all was my friend the Reverend Strauch, who was serving a church in Fort Collins, Colorado. Every time I visited the Strauchs they had a candidate that would make a suitable minister's wife. At last they sprung a surprise on me. They invited to dinner a young schoolteacher who was attending the summer semester at the agricultural college and was rooming with their neighbors. It so happened that the young woman's name was Amelia Ament, and she was the daughter of John Ament, who was a member of Strauch's church at the time I served the church in Proctor during the summer months.

Amelia and I had so many things in common that we were naturally drawn to each other. She had lost both her parents during the flu epidemic. They had both been buried on the same day. Dialogue between us came easily, and our relationship gained momentum. We agreed that our lives belonged together. I realized that married, I would have to abandon all hope of ever returning to Russia again, but that fact had already become clear to me.

The Strauchs were beaming when we broke the news to them that they had at long last succeeded in making a match.

"Bill," I said, "I am a poor man and can't afford to come up with the marriage fee. But will you do us the honor and tie the knot?"

"With the greatest of pleasure," was his answer. "The fact that I brought you together is reward enough for me."

Another congregational minister, Dr. Allingham, and his wife were invited to serve as best man and matron of honor; and the ceremony took place in the parsonage.

For the wedding feast we all decided to drive to Denver and find a Chinese restaurant. Dr. Allingham, who enjoyed making everybody laugh, ordered egg foo yong. He said he liked the sound of it and persuaded us to follow suit. The party was in a jovial mood.

After getting back to Fort Collins, Amelia and I decided that I would return to my church in Cheyenne and she would stay to finish the semester, which was to last only two more weeks.

My congregation was delighted when I broke the news to them and announced that no more would they have to be concerned about the bachelorhood of their minister and that he had married not only a schoolteacher but a woman who would be able to fill the job of organist for the church.

My friend the conspirator, who had thought it a good idea to put temptation in the way of his minister by having a widow visit his apartment, sat in the back pew and with a wide grin on his face silently went through a hand-clapping motion. After the service he came up to me and whispered, "Now we don't have to tempt you any more, Reverend."

My task for the following week was to find suitable living quarters and get everything ready for the new life ahead of us. The cottage I rented was only a short distance from the church. The only recommendation this little four-room cottage belonging to a Mexican had was the low rent. Acquiring the needed furniture I left for the time when Amelia could help in selecting it.

There was an Orthodox Jewish Zionist who had a secondhand furniture store. He and I often discussed Zionism and had become good friends. He offered to let us have all the furniture, including a mattress, for reasonable monthly payments.

The long-awaited day when we would be able to enter our home had come. The happiness that we had the first night, however, took second place to the nightmare we were to experience. Indeed, it was a honeymoon nightmare! Around midnight we were both awakened by severe itching. Almost simultaneously we guessed that it could mean one thing--bed-bugs! We both jumped out of bed. Having had previous encounters with these little night raiders, I knew that they were strictly nocturnal operators and detested light. I said to Amelia, Now, when I get ready to throw back the cover, you switch on the light. I was ready for them, and the minute the light flicked on, I pounced on them like a cat, squashing them left and right as they tried to scamper for cover. We had to sleep the rest of the night on the floor.

It was a night neither of us ever forgot--and a night we would not have traded for the most luxurious suite in any metropolitan hotel.

The following morning we found that the habitat of these little pests was not the mattress alone. There were some who had squatters' rights long before we moved in. They came crawling out of the woodwork everywhere--the window sills, the moldings, the doorjambs. There were so many bugs in our love nest that I suggested we stake it down, lest these inhabitants get together and move it away.

Amelia had me get some coal oil, and for the next few days we both became exterminators. I was proud of my wife and the way she rose to the challenge. She would be a good minister's wife.

We both enjoyed the church work. Life had certainly taken on a new dimension. The fact that we were contributing toward people's happiness was indeed rewarding. To see children responding to the teaching of Jesus was heartwarming.

Amelia was a good piano and organ player. She was also by far the best kindergarten teacher in the organization. Children worshipped her. Her specialty was working with beginners. Every Bible story had to be acted out. Everyone in her class had to become an actor. She would assign the different roles and proceed to reenact Bible stories. She would always come home with some choice and mirthful stories to tell on her little thespians. When they acted out the story of the Good Samaritan, the little boy playing the part of the Good Samaritan was also the son of the garbage collector. So after he was finished tending the prostrate victim by the roadside, he gently kicked him in the side and said, "Now, go and be a god garbage collector." Apparently, his daddy's occupation was for him the most honorable one he could think of.

During our brief stay in Cheyenne I was ordained. As a full-fledged minister, I was now in line for a bigger church. We were fortunate to receive a call from one of our leading churches in the Pacific Northwest, from Saint Matthew's in Odessa, Washington. Naturally, we were glad to accept.

Our friend, the Jewish furniture dealer, was glad and kind enough to take back the furniture, minus the bugs, and did not charge us extra. All it cost us was a slight rental fee.

When we were getting ready for our trip out west, our first problem was to raise money to pay for the moving. It was

Amelia who came up with the solution. Her parents had left her some railroad stock, which she was willing to cash in so that we could buy a car. We bought a new Chrysler coupe and got ready to head west.

Our first stop was Billings, Montana. Uncle Fred was pastor of a church there, and we stayed with them overnight. Arriving at uncle's parsonage, Amelia complained of nausea. I suggested that perhaps she was carsick. Aunt Rose gave a sly smile and shook her head. "No," she said. "I think it is something more than that. It is possible that someone is on his way to join the family, and it could be Paul Junior." Amelia nodded her head in agreement.

Was it really true? I couldn't believe it. Suddenly I was sailing on a cloud, thinking that soon I would become a father. Before leaving Billings I assumed the role of strict disciplinarian and gave Amelia orders: "Now, you just put your foot down early, and don't let that youngster get away with any funny business." She just laughed and said that if he had the disposition of his father, there would be no use in putting a foot down.

Continuing our journey, we reached Idaho the following day. Passing by some apple orchards, Amelia developed a craving for apples. I had to stop and ask one of the owners for permission to pick some. The farmer's wife met me at the door; and when I explained my predicament to her, she was very much amused and even helped me to select choice apples. Returning to the car with enough apples to last us for the rest of the trip, we drove happily on, glad that Amelia did not crave pickles and ice cream.

We had not gone many miles when we developed engine trouble. Never having owned a car before, I had no idea what could be wrong. Steam was hissing out on both sides of the block. We barely made it to the garage. The mechanic there discovered that it was a blown gasket and would take about four hours to repair.

Now we had another problem. With only thirty dollars left to take us to our destination, how would we be able to pay for the repairs? Again, I had an angel resting on my shoulder. The owner of the garage, who was about my age and had just recently been married himself, was sympathetic. He even took us out for lunch and picked up the tab. I offered to leave him my wristwatch as security, but he would not have it. "Send me the money whenever you can afford it," he said.

What a pleasant feeling it gives one to find kindness and consideration where sometimes one least expects it. Needless to say, this debt was one of the first that we paid.

Things went well the rest of our journey. Around three o'clock we hit the sagebrush country beyond Davenport, Washington, and were beginning to watch for road signs pointing to Odessa. At last, there is was: eight miles to Odessa. It was a wonderful feeling that within a few minutes we would reach our new home. Before we had reached the outskirts of the town another little episode happened. Amelia called my attention to a package lying ahead of us in the middle of the road. The speed of the car took me a few feet beyond the package, but I stopped to investigate. Approaching the package, I noticed that it was an inner tube, nicely wrapped and tied; at the same time there was in evidence a string leading from the package down the side of the road. Not a stranger to practical jokes, my suspicion was aroused. I stared at it for a moment, making no move to pick it up, then quickly stepped on the string. There was a sharp tug, and the string broke. Unconcerned, I picked up the package and started for the car. Then I heard the plaintive cry of a couple of youngsters: "Hey, mister, aren't you going to give us back our tube?" "No." I said. "Finders keepers." And I stepped into the car. Driving on a short distance, I threw the package out of the window. They both raced to retrieve it.

The real climax to the episode came on the following Sunday morning in Sunday school. In the second pew from the front I saw two giggling boys, the same practical jokesters that we had seen a couple of day before. They kept eyeing me, red-faced and a bit embarrassed. Delivering my message to the school, I started by thanking them all for the wonderful reception that had given us, even going so far as sending two little boys to meet us out on the road as we were driving in. Naturally, I had to reveal the inner tube episode. The whole auditorium broke out with spontaneous laughter. We had made the right kind of impression. Everybody felt relaxed and jovial. The little byplay had accomplished a useful mission.

## Chapter 16
## ODESSA, WASHINGTON

OUR MINISTRY IN ODESSA began without tension. We felt fortunate to have our first call after ordination come from one of the leading churches in the West.

Odessa was a church town. There were altogether six churches in this town of 3,000. There were two German congregational churches, an English Congregational church, a Lutheran church, a Baptist church and a Catholic church.

Saint Matthew's Church and its parsonage were located on the main highway leaving town for the coast. Most of the members were farmers. It was rather handy for the parishioners because they could stop by either coming in or leaving the city and bring the minister's family some good homemade German sausage, butter, and eggs to keep us well supplied.

Between the German churches there was always a friendly rivalry. The Saint Matthew's people were primarily Volga Germans, and the members of the sister church were Russian-German originally coming from the Odessa district in southern Russia.

The pastor of the other church was a schoolmate of mine, Rev. A. Delabar. We enjoyed each other's company and did a lot of fishing and hunting together. The cluster of lakes around the town were all well stocked with bass and perch. In the wintertime it was always a festive occasion to take part in the "rabbit drives." Lined up like an invading army, the hunters were lined up, marching across the sagebrush countryside. The explosions of gunshots sounded as if there were a battle going on. After the drive the animals were put on a truck and sent to Spokane to some charitable organization.

To heighten our joy in Odessa, Amelia made our happiness complete by giving birth to our first child. Loretta Elaine made us a family--and what a difference that made!

Saint Matthew's had one distinction, namely, the best choir in town. Several very competent pianists in the congregation made choir directing comparatively easy. One musician in particular, thirteen-year-old Evelyn Walter, was very talented. It was a delight to watch her perform on the keyboard. She tossed her long curls while gliding her fingers over the keys, looking almost in all directions but that of the keys. It was no wonder she was always in demand at state conventions as a soloist.

We decided to put on the cantata "King David." The night of the presentation standing room was at a premium. People had come from Ritzville and other neighboring towns to listen to it. The local newspaper gave us a glowing review and characterized it as: "the best musical entertainment ever presented in Odessa." Of course, all the choir members were happy and proud of the recognition.

The fact that the parsonage was on the

highway also brought us many out-of-town visitors who stopped in on their way to the coast. One of my greatest surprises came when I answered the door and there stood my old benefactor, Dr. Fath. He was on his way to a convention of astronomers in southern California. I was especially delighted when I saw him take out a Havana cigar to light it. It gave us a chance to discuss and laugh over an incident that had occurred during our Redfield days.

It happened that there were certain rules passed by the faculty regarding dating. Some of the students who had steady girl friends objected to the rules being too strict. I, on the other hand, was much in favor of them, just to be different. One of the students was heard to remark, "Paul is for campus rules and is the first one to break the rules. I am going to report that he has been seen smoking cigars on campus, which is against the rules." When I heard about the impending snitching, I immediately decided to beat him to it and report myself. Dr. Fath was in the office and as usual was sucking on something that appeared to be a "breath killer" of some kind, although at the time no one knew that he, too, smoked on the sly. I told him that I had heard someone was coming in to report me for having smoked on the campus. I admitted that it was so. He looked at me over his glasses and smiled and said something to me that made me admire him all the more: "Paul, I don't consider it wrong that you take a smoke once in a while, but I think it is wrong that you let them catch you at it."

Well, we reviewed many Redfield experiences and enjoyed laughing about them.

Another visitor that always made his headquarters at our home whenever he came to town collecting money was a Hindu missionary by the name of Sadhu John Nelson Christananta. Every so often he would tour the States, speaking in German churches to collect money to support his work in India. The first time he came to our home he had carried a small rug rolled up under his arm. I asked him why he was carrying that rug along. He explained that it was a habit that stemmed back to the days when he was a Moslem. It was a prayer rug. He was such a friendly man, always smiling and displaying a set of flashing white teeth. We got to be such good friends that we indulged in joshing each other. He accused me of being more of a Hindu than he was. "All you need," he would say, "is a turban." In his Hindu regalia, he reminded one of an apostle.

On his last trip he decided to visit France. We had all forgotten about him when suddenly after six months he appeared again. It was midnight when he came to our door. I could hardly believe my eyes when I saw the transformation that had taken place. The apostolic garment was gone. He was garbed in an extremely modern suit and vest and, of all things, a pair of gray spats. The only item left from his former regalia was a bright orange turban. I said to him, "Sadhu, it appears to me that Paris has left more of an impression on you than you have on Paris." Again the toothy smile displaying the white ivories. Our beds were all taken, and he insisted on sleeping on the sofa. The next morning at the breakfast table I asked him whether he was familiar with the yoga. "Oh, yes, indeed," he said. "I have been practicing it. Why?" "Well, in that case," I answered, "I need offer no apology for the lumpy sofa since you no doubt slept well." Again one of his jovial chuckles as he called me a rascal.

There was one habit that he had to which I took exception. Despite his eloquence in preaching, he could not refrain from downgrading American missionaries. He called them bookkeepers who were only interested in numbers indicating their measure of success. I offered a slight reprimand, stating that criticizing the Americans was hardly conducive to creating a charitable audience. But it was nice knowing him.

Another frequent visitor was Dr. Seil. He was at one time president of Redfield College and during his retirement served a small church in Washington not far from us.

Having suffered a severe heart attack, he had been confined to a Spokane hospital. After he had been discharged we invited him to stay at our home during his convalescence. A local doctor came regularly to check on him. The one instruction the doctor gave was that he should keep his feet elevated--something I constantly had to remind him of. Finally the doctor called me aside and told me that in his opinion I should make an effort to persuade him to go to his nearest relatives, if he had any, as quickly as possible. It was a delicate situation for me. I did not tell him that in the doctor's opinion he had only a very short time left, but instead managed to get the address of his only daughter, who was married to a professor in southern California. I wrote to the lady and explained the situation to her. She sent a telegram: "Please put papa on the next train--we will take care of him." When I told him that his daughter wanted him to come and live with them, he was so happy he had tears in his eyes. We put him on the train, and two weeks later received the message that he had passed away.

Since he was almost penniless when he stayed with us, his only way of doing something for us was to insist that we accept some of his books. One set I cherish is Oswald Spengler's *The Decline of the West (Der Untergang des Abendlandes)*. These were some of the books that Hitler ordered burned. I cherish them very much.

The town had two medical doctors, a dentist, a lawyer, and a newspaper editor. I always enjoyed discussions with the lawyer since he had the most time to spare. He was a retired judge and wanted to take it easy during his late years without retiring altogether. He prided himself on being an agnostic and an iconoclast, which gave me a chance to defend the very dogmas I used to question.

One Sunday morning, to my great surprise, I saw our agnostic in church. I felt honored since he had repeated on several occasions that he had no use for the church and its preachers. Monday morning I stopped by his office to get his reaction. "You know," he said to me, "I must confess that I was able to swallow what you had to say. But tell me, why are you always defending Jesus? During your entire sermon you were defending your client. You had Jesus before the bar, and you were arguing and pleading for a favorable verdict. I did not realize that he had to be defended, since those in the audience were all on his side. Is it possible that the judge whom you were trying to convince was yourself?"

At the time I was reluctant to admit it, but I found out as time went on that the old judge had clear insight into human nature. I had always had a struggle going on within me between the practical and dogmatic aspect of religion.

We loved our work in Odessa. The minister there was more than just a preacher; he was considered by every member a friend.

Another high point in our lives came when Amelia, four years after the birth of Loretta, presented me with another precious bundle.

We named her Dorothy Lee. Naturally there was a good deal of fussing over the newborn baby. The fact that Dorothy was the center of attention did not go down well with Loretta. She was such a sensitive child. While everyone was gathered around the baby, Loretta all of a sudden was nowhere to be seen. I went looking for her. On the steps behind the church I found the little four-year-old, a picture of sadness. She was resting her chin in both her palms. Guessing what ailed her, I spoke to her: "Honey, why are you out here all alone? Don't you like your baby sister?" Keeping her pose and without looking up, she muttered, "I guess nobody wants me."

I picked her up and hugged her, "Of course, we want you," I said, pressing her to my heart. "We just thought --your mommy and I--that you would like to have a little playmate. We love you both just the same." That assurance performed an instant miracle. She had heard the magic words "We love you" and that changed everything. Often during my ministry I thought how many broken hearts could be mended if only those three words were spoken more often. To be hated is not nearly as bad as not being loved.

The two children, growing up, helped to deepen the roots of affection for the people. The children soon acquired several grandpas and grandmas. One lived only a block away from the parsonage. One day he stopped at our home just to relate a lovely incident that had taken place several days before. It seemed that he had been sick in bed. Someone was knocking at the front door. Grandma went to answer. When she opened the door, she found Loretta standing there in her mother's high-heeled shoes, a shawl draped around her shoulders, requesting that she be let in to visit the sick grandpa. She went into the sickroom, sat down on the chair beside the bed, and sat there without saying a word. After a while she got up and left, apparently satisfied that she had performed her duty. It impressed the old man so that he had to make a special trip to tell us about it. That child was never idle. Her little friend and daily companion, little Harriet, lived close by. Whenever we wanted Loretta to come home, I would just stick my head out the back door and give a shrill whistle. Within a few minutes she would be running down the hill towards home. The little busybody was always inquisitive and full of questions. After a funeral I always had to answer questions like "Daddy, why were the people crying? Why were they feeling so bad?"

One day Loretta and Dorothy crawled up on the sofa to sit beside me. Dorothy was now two and a half years old and took an active part in the conversation. Again the questions about funerals and death. I asked them, "If you had to die, how would you like to die?" The little one had her answer ready first: "I would like to have a goat chew off my head." That was Dorothy's best solution for a quick death. It was now Loretta's turn to answer. She had a faraway look on her face, as if she had to make up her mind about dying. Finally she very plaintively said, "Daddy, I think I want to die of old age." Assuring her that her choice was the right one and she would live to be very old made her happy.

It gave us much joy to see the children grow up. They were so totally different in temperament and nature. One was an extrovert, and the other an introvert. Loretta was forever asking questions and showing her feelings; the little one was quiet and independent but outspoken and serious. If I wanted her to sit on my lap and she had other things on her mind, she would just jerk her arm away from me and say, "Don't bother me!"

Serving the congregation in Odessa deepened our love for the ministry. It was an active and peaceful period.

The stock market crash was the beginning of hard times. Wheat prices dropped to an all time low. Farmers did not have enough money to run their farms. The minister's salary was slow in coming if it came at all. A widow who was unable to pay her church dues brought us a cedar chest that her son had made in manual training, and offered it in lieu of her church dues. We accepted it. People were becoming poor and desperate.

To compound our personal hardships, we received letters from abroad telling us of hunger and starvation, and begging for help. Out of our meager income, we set a certain amount aside every month to send to my mother.

A letter I received from the president of the Krasnodar Technological Institute made me a unique offer. He stated that he knew my brother and my mother and also knew that I was sending them food every month. He said that if I would be willing to act as the institute's agent, ordering certain laboratory equipment from a firm in Austria, and paying for these orders in dollars, they would see to it that my mother would receive the equal amount every month from the institute. They needed the equipment, and it was only available here. The government, however, did not permit any money to leave Russia at the time.

It was a good arrangement. Only one

time did they fail to pay mother. When I withheld payment to the firm in Austria, I again received a pleading letter from Dr. Alexeev, asking me to please resume my service. He apologized for the inconvenience caused my mother, but added that it was due to the fact that mother had moved and failed to leave her address.

It had not been much that we could spare monthly, but we learned later that it had been enough to keep them from starving. I considered it another sign that destiny had had a hand in sending me to America.

The congregation was in arrears with my salary. With no money coming in, we had difficulty feeding the family of four and helping the destitute abroad. We had to come to a decision. The congregation did not want us to leave, but we had no choice. It was a sad parting. Just how much the people thought of the minister and his family was demonstrated after the Depression, when again they wanted us to come back.

## Chapter 17
### HASTINGS, NEBRASKA

WE ACCEPTED A CALL FROM Hastings, Nebraska. When Dr. Obenhaus learned of it, he was quite disturbed. In his opinion, the field was too difficult for a young minister. It was one of the first German churches that was bilingual. Preaching had to be done in both languages. It meant that a minister's work load was almost doubled. Besides, the church had a reputation of changing ministers quite frequently on that account. According to the good doctor, "You are too young to be jeopardizing your health at such an early age." But it was a challenge that I could not resist.

The church members were all city dwellers and lived in the neighborhood of the church. They were employed by either the railroad or the local furniture factory. Several of the employees were talented craftsmen and did some expert wood carving. They were of the same origin as the Odessa people; some even came from the same village in the Volga district. The fact that they had been city dwellers and a lot of the young people attended the local college gave them a better than average sophistication.

The parsonage was a two-story colonial with ample space. Amelia was very happy to be moving into such a lovely home. The backyard contained a good-sized vegetable garden, giving her plenty of opportunity to use her green thumb.

The children had no trouble finding friends. The family next door, by the name of Baker, was a large family. Their two preschoolers either were at our home or our two girls were at theirs. Dorothy, who always had an appetite, had a friend in Mr. Baker. He was section foremen and carried a dinner bucket to work with him. On returning home he would turn the bucket over to Dorothy, and she went through it like a little raccoon. Baker always managed to leave something in the bucket that she liked, either some fruit or a candy bar.

Loretta was in her first year at school. She was still "Miss Tender Heart."

A lady living close to the school came to tell us about a scene she had witnessed. It seemed that some children were picking on a little Mexican girl and were hitting her. Loretta went to the child's rescue, put her arms around her to shield her, and told the other children to leave the girl alone and not to be so mean. "You should have seen the way your little girl stood up to those little tormentors. You would have been proud of her. "

Dr. Obenhaus's warning had been justified. I had called a church board meeting to convene in the parsonage. While we were waiting for the rest of the members, two of those already present started a discussion relative to something that was supposed to have happened ten years prior. The discussion turned into an argument, and they kept getting louder and obviously angry. When they began to insult each other, I rapped for order. They were still glaring at each other, and I thought a little lecture was in order. I said, "What I am going to say to you now may have a bearing as to the future of my ministry here. What we have just witnessed reminds me of a Russian nobleman and his pet hunting dog. The dog had gotten so old and feeble that he was of no use anymore; but, having served his master for so many years, he was permitted to live. The dog, however, had one bad habit. Whenever he had nothing to gnaw on, he would unearth an old cow tail that he had buried and drag it right into the kitchen. It seems to me that some of you enjoy digging up unpleasant incidents of past history whenever there is nothing current to fight about, just to antagonize each other. Now, if you want me to continue as pastor of this church, this bickering and quarreling has got to stop. You are Christians and grown men, not children."

They were all stunned. Total silence for a while. Then one of the debaters got up, extended his hand, and said, "Forgive me, brother, it was my fault!" The other one, not to be outdone in remorse, countered with, "No brother, it was my fault!"

Again, I had to break in. "Now, let's not start the argument all over again, deciding whose fault it was. Your confessions are commendable." On a happy note, I concluded by saying, "I think we can now proceed with the business at hand." Everybody laughed, and the meeting progressed without further disturbance.

A current of fresh air had suddenly cleared the air. Everybody went away in good spirits. The effect of that board meeting was in evidence in every business meeting thereafter. The moment anyone even suggested or brought up something the least bit controversial, a voice was sure to be heard: "Let's not drag in any cow tails!" It would immediately have a calming effect, and the meeting would proceed without disturbance.

Dr. Obenhaus paid us a visit just to see

how we were getting along. We were walking over to the church to look things over. Some city sewer workers had dug up the ground in front of the church and had left a mound resembling a freshly covered grave. The doctor wanted to know what had happened. Remembering his earlier warning that the field was too tough for a young minister, I said to him, "We just had a business meeting and had to bury one of the troublemakers." He laughed and answered that perhaps he should suggest that to some of the other congregations. He was a good sport and enjoyed a bit of levity.

Back at the parsonage, we got down to some serious discussion. He listened attentively as I outlined my working schedule. Besides the two sermons, I had to speak to the Sunday school, the prayer meeting in the afternoon, and the Christian Endeavor meeting in the evening. The sermons always had to be bilingual. After the German had to follow a short sermon in English. The old man shook his head and responded, "Sooner or later you will have to pay the price for carrying such a schedule." I told him that by the time I came to my last service of the day I often fell asleep in the chair while waiting a few minutes in the study for the last bell, and a deacon had to shake me, reminding me that it was time for the pulpit. "Promise me," the good doctor pleaded, "that if I find you a different field, you will accept." I promised.

Hastings taxed our strength, but we still managed to be happy there. We loved the people, and one of their redeeming features was the talented and competent younger group.

The choir was directed by one of the young men, and I merely had to be present to keep order. In that respect we sometimes had some pleasant diversions. Our vivacious organist, who was the leader of the group and could chew gum in time with her playing, also was astute enough to observe that whenever I was displeased with something, I took out my dollar watch and started to wind it. Knowing that that was the signal that a verbal storm was to break loose, she would whisper, "Simmer down, you guys. He's winding his watch!"

A violin teacher came to the neighborhood soliciting pupils. When I told him that our older daughter was only six years old, he asked to see her. He looked at her hands and assured us that she would be able to start lessons on a half-sized instrument. Knowing that she loved music, we enrolled her.

After she had taken lessons for several months he had me come into his studio. He said, "I want to show you something." He then told Loretta to turn her back to him. He picked up his violin and sounded a note, then asked the child what note it was, and she identified it correctly. Then he continued, by pleading, "By all means, never let that child give up the violin. She is a natural musician."

She advanced much faster than he had anticipated. We all took advantage of the child's good nature and agreeableness, and kept encouraging her. It was never a problem to get her to practice her lessons.

Sometimes her arm was so tired that she was inclined to lower the instrument. Then daddy would say, "Up with the arms!" The response came without complaint.

After the first year the professor put on a recital in the form of a contest. To our great surprise, Loretta won the blue ribbon and cup. Amelia and I were very proud of our children, and that fact was reflected in the attitude of the parishioners. Someone was heard to say, "These children will never have to feel sorry that they are a preacher's kids." While Loretta made us happy by displaying her musical talent, the two-year-old Dorothy made her conquest in a different manner. She was chubby and had a heavy head of hair. The fact that she was always so serious and independent made some people all the more anxious to pick her up, for one was never sure what she would say.

The Sunday school superintendent, a Mr. Herbst, took the family for an automobile ride to show us the sights. When the car hit a bump and caused it to jump a bit, it was Dorothy who spoke up and said, "Herbst--not so hard!" Well that struck Herbst so funny that he could not stop laughing. She had established an image as an innocent and outspoken child whose insults were considered compliments.

Once, during an evening service while I was up on the chancel, preaching, I noticed a commotion in the congregation where Amelia was sitting with Dorothy's head in her lap. People kept looking over at Amelia and laughing. After the service I inquired about the cause of the disturbance. One of the ladies volunteered the explanation: "You should have heard your little touslehead. You startled her by getting a little loud, whereupon she raised her sleepy head and said in her low voice 'I wish my daddy would shut up!' " Could be she expressed the opinion of many others.

At another time the family went for a ride out to the insane asylum, which was not very far from the parsonage. As we kept circling around, we passed the building housing the more violent inmates. A woman appeared at the window, raised her dress, and called down to us, "Look me over, cowboy!" Amelia and I both laughed and did not think that the children noticed it. That night as we were were getting the children ready for bed, I was undressing the little one to put on her nightie, when she jumped up and down on the bed and shouted, "Look me ova, tow boy!"

In connection with that institution I had another memorable experience. As a member of the Ministerial Association, it was my turn to conduct the monthly service for the inmates. After the service some of the patients stepped up to shake hands. One of them spoke to me in a very serious tone: "I liked your sermon; but what you were preaching brought me out here."

It was a compliment that caused me to reflect. My colleagues were quite amused when I gave my report at the next meeting.

A church in Lincoln, Nebraska, was host to the state conference. I happened to be on the program to preach a sermon. During the service an elderly woman caught my attention by intently looking at me and smiling. I was beginning to think that she knew me; yet I could not place her. The minister of the church came to me after the service with an invitation to the lady's home. When we arrived at her home, she met us at the door. Her first question was, "Was your father's name Gottlieb?" I answered in the affirmative. "And was your grandfather's name Gottlieb, too?" Again my answer was in the affirmative. At that point she threw her arms around my neck, kissing me, and said, "You are my Paulusha!" By that time, I had guessed her identity. I replied, "And you are Madneta." As a child I had not been able to pronounce her name, Magdalena. She was the maid who had taken care of the children in our family. As a matter of fact, she had been adopted by my parents. When I was only three years old she had gotten married, had received a dowry from my father, and had migrated to America. It was a touching reunion. I had actually met a member of our family.

The Hastings church had some skilled artisans in the furniture factory. One of the men made me a beautiful bookcase of quarter-sawed oak. Not to be outdone, another member made one to match it but with an added feature--pigeonholes for filing things. A third one made a table and chairs for the children. And still another came with a toy dresser. These items are today enjoyed by the grandchildren.

Contrary to all expectations, the Hastings people brought us many happy moments. The only unhappy news came from abroad. People were still starving, and new hardships had been imposed upon them. The Communist government made its final attempt to enforce collective farming, and those who resisted were imprisoned or exiled.

The winters in Nebraska were severe, and the summers sultry and hot. Often we had to sleep on the floor by the open door. We also experienced a frightening tornado while there. When we saw the ominous dark funnel approaching, we took the children across the street to seek shelter in the neighbor's cellar. When we asked the old widow, who was a member of our church, for permission to enter her cellar, she was glad to accommodate us, but added, "Reverend, if the good Lord wants you, he can get you down there, too." Apparently she did not believe in trying to run away from danger. I answered her, "If the good Lord wants me, he knows where he can get me." It was not too long before she joined us, laughing and remarking, "I thought over what you said, and it made a lot of sense. Why make it easy for the Lord?" Her sense of humor was refreshing.

When it was all over, the streets were a terrible sight. Every imaginable kind of debris was there, blown-over trees blocking the streets. It was almost as bad as the hailstorm I had witnessed years ago in Canada. There were stories of people out on the road leaving their cars standing, and seeking safety by clinging to the trunks of trees.

Needless to say, we were still in love

with the West and always had the desire to return there if at all possible.

We received a call from Biola, California. We rather suspected that Dr. Obenhaus had followed through on his promise. We accepted the call. Our two little ambassadors lost no time in spreading the news. They were excited, telling everybody that we were moving to a country where it was never cold and always summer, where there was a lot of fresh fruit--apples, pears, grapes, oranges, and even "crowberries" (strawberries), as Dorothy put it. Again, a ministry that had added to our store of happy memories had come to an end.

## Chapter 18
### BIOLA, CALIFORNIA

OUR MOVE FROM HASTINGS to Biola was a bit more involved. While in Hastings we had acquired some choice pieces of furniture that Amelia would not part with at any price. We had to engage a large moving van to take our household goods. The van left a day ahead of us to make sure it would arrive there before we did.

This time our trip was sheer pleasure. We had a four-door sedan and a couple of bouncing, bubbling children keeping us looking in all directions.

On the fourth day, around noon, we arrived in Biola. The sight that greeted us was most impressive. The church building was of Spanish mission architecture. At the entrance there were four colonnades. The churchyard was a veritable park. Several rows of shade trees lined the parking strips. The children could hardly wait to get out of the car and go on a treasure hunt. Soon they came running from behind the parsonage, all excited and shouting, "Mom and daddy, come and see what we have found--grapes hanging down from the roof of the house." What they had discovered was a grape arbor running the entire length of the house, about seven feet away, with the overhead trellis attached to the base of the roof, thus permitting clusters of grapes to hang overhead and on the side. That was our private little vineyard. To heighten the children's enthusiasm still more, they found a fig tree outside the entrance door at the back of the house.

Peering through the windows, we noticed that all our furniture had been unpacked and arranged inside the parsonage. All we needed was the key.

The neighbor across the street had seen us arrive and hurried over to bring us the key. The house was immaculate, and we could not have done better ourselves. The refrigerator was even stocked with food. All Amelia had to do was to light the butane stove and prepare our meal.

After we had eaten and were relaxing

in the living room, we saw a car drive up. Four men got out. They seemed in a very jovial mood. One of them, a mountain of a man and obviously the spokesman, was walking ahead of the rest as they came to the front door. They stopped just in front of the door and lined up like a squad of soldiers ready for inspection, whispering and laughing. I opened the door.

The big man spoke: "Reverend Kalmbach, we are the church board members and have come to welcome you and your family. My name is Wolf." Then he indicated, nodding to his companions, that they were to say their names one after the other.

The next one introduced himself: "My name is Baer."

"My name if Fox" and lastly:

"My name is Haas" (German for "rabbit").

By this time I had gotten the drift of their little play and went right along with it. It was apparent that I had in front of me a group of men with a healthy sense of humor. It was now time for me to show my reaction: "I knew that the name of the church was Friedens Kirche (Peace Church), but I had no idea that I was to be the pastor of the church that had already reached the millennium. Certainly a congregation where a wolf, a bear, a fox and a rabbit can get along so peacefully must be an ideal congregation. Please come in!" They came in laughing, obviously glad that their new minister also had a sense of humor to match their own.

The people of the church really lived up to its name. These people also came from the Volga district but seemed of an entirely different breed. They had come from the meadow side of the Volga River and were endowed with a spirit of friendliness that we had so far not encountered anywhere.

The people we had had in our previous churches had been kind and hospitable, some of them quite modern and proud. But these people had a special sparkle That could not escape one's attention. It was the same wherever we would meet. Whether in church or at some other activity, they always found reasons to make each other laugh.

There was one brother in particular, in appearance like a big Buddha, who, more than anyone, loved to laugh. Everybody knew that, and they always found a way to set him off. Once he went into his act, gasping for breath, his face turning crimson and his fat neck swelling over his shirt collar, it seemed that at any moment he would be rolling on the ground. He had everybody join in with him. He also had a reputation for being an excellent winemaker, and whenever there was a church business meeting a number of the members could be seen periodically making trips to his car to caress a jug. The meeting, however, always went off smoothly, without any disturbance. They never overdid their indulgence and frowned on anyone who did.

Our winemaker had a unique experience that the whole countryside was talking about. It happened one morning when he came out to feed his pigs. He found them sitting on their haunches, weaving back and forth. Thinking that they were all sick, he administered first aid by resorting to some old remedy, that of bleeding. These pigs had to be bled, he thought, and he set to work by bobbing their ears.

When the mailman arrived to make some delivery, he noticed all the hogs had bobbed ears, and to satisfy his curiosity asked why all the ears had been cut off. Listening to the explanation, he noticed a big pile of grape husks nearby with a fork in it. "Did you feed your pigs some of these husks?" he asked. When the winemaker answered that these crushed husks made good hog feed, the mailman doubled over, laughing, and gasped, "If cutting the pig's ears off was a remedy for what ailed them, my ears should have been cut off, too. Your pigs were stoned. These husks are fermented and have a high content of alcohol."

This episode was too good for the mailman to keep to himself. Everyone getting mail on that day was also treated to a choice piece of gossip.

For a while the poor man was beset with telephone calls from his neighbors.

All claimed that they had sick pigs and asked if he would come and apply his remedy. No one enjoyed the joke more than our jolly winemaker himself.

Not far from the parsonage there was a raisin-packing house. It was infested with rats. These rodents invaded our garage and utility room. One of the church members came over and brought me a 22-caliber rifle. He asked me whether I knew how to handle a gun. When I told him that I was quite familiar with fire arms, he assured me that in this case I could become a rat exterminator.

"All you need," he said, "is a strong flashlight and the rifle."

I was to go into the utility room after dark and direct the beam of light at the rafters just below the roof. The light would momentarily blind the pests, and they could easily be picked off with the rifle. My hunting expedition was successful, but only for a few nights. It seems that rats sometimes learn faster than humans. The minute the light hit them, they associated it with the demise of one of their relatives and would immediately scurry for cover. After a while, the ones that were still alive decided to leave on their own accord.

Rats were not the only pests we had to contend with. Woodpeckers and black widow spiders were a nuisance. The woodpeckers started their work early in the morning. They kept chopping holes into the church. Seeing one of them starting to chop a hole right about the chancel, I went for my rifle. They shot missed, but the bullet went right in through the hole our little lumberjack had started. Immediately I suspected the worst and ran into the church to see what had happened. Right above the chancel was the hole, and there was plaster all over the pulpit. I cleaned it up as well as I could and even tried to repair the hole. Every Sunday morning, as I approached the pulpit, my eyes automatically traveled over to the bullet hole.

When I told one of my colleagues, my former schoolmate, of the incident, he shook his head and said, "Paul, I am not surprised. In seminary days you used to enjoy sniping at some of the old church doctrines, and now you are blasting holes in the church building itself."

The fact that the church had the appearance of a Spanish mission caused many Mexican field hands to stop on their way to the fields to kneel in front of the altar and pray.

When the sexton found out about this practice, he locked the church doors. That was not my concept of spreading Christianity. I went and opened the doors again and left them unlocked. One day the sexton mildly reprimanded me and stated, "Don't you know, Reverend, that we have many Bibles lying around in church? Aren't you afraid they might carry some away?" My reply was that that would be a theft that could be forgiven. If anyone had so much a need of a Bible that he would steal one, it would still be a missionary act. To keep a church locked to prevent people from coming in does not seem consistent with the church's mission. The church stayed unlocked from then on.

Sometimes I took the family to San Francisco or Oakland. We would stop on the way and take the children into a Catholic cathedral that stood beside the road. They were so impressed that one of them said, "Daddy, why aren't we Catholic?" I answered, "When you are old enough to decide for yourself and want to become a Catholic, you will have my blessing." Fifteen years later Dorothy was admitted to the Catholic church. She also attended a Catholic university and was graduated as a nurse.

There were six German churches in and around Fresno. The fellowship between ministers and their families was commendable. Every so often the ministers and their wives would get together at one of the parsonages for a sociable afternoon. These meetings were stimulating and helpful in renewing one's enthusiasm and strength to carry on the Lord's work.

The Cross Church, in Fresno, was, so to speak, the "mother hen." It had a membership of around two thousand. Its pastor, the Reverend Paul Krumbein, was a dear old man. He was widowed and had a family of eight. We all looked upon him as our dean. He never failed to visit us two or three times during the month. We were all disappointed when he announced his retirement, which was due to ill health and advanced age.

The question that was on everyone's mind was, Who would get the call from Cross? Some of their board members came out to call on me. The purpose of their visit was to find out whether I would accept a call. We were happy where we were. Nevertheless, the temptation was too great to simply say no. I promised that I would consider it.

Several weeks went by, and nothing was heard until one day I met one of the board members in the Fresno marketplace. I asked him about the church's decision. He apologized and explained: "Some of the Biola board members, having learned of Cross's intention to give the call, came in to meet with our board. Their purpose was to dissuade us from giving that call, and they threatened that if we took their minister away they would break off the fellowship between the two churches. So we agreed not to deprive them of their minister."

It was a compliment to think that my board members would go to such lengths to keep me, but at the time it made me very angry. How dare they interfere with the course of my life? While I was still in that angry mood, I received a call that very week from the Zion Church, in Portland, Oregon. We did something for which we could never quite forgive ourselves thereafter. We accepted the call. It was a regrettable mistake and should not have happened; and had the call come at least a week later, we would not have been so hasty.

My announcement to the Friedens Church that I had accepted a call from another church came as a complete surprise. The people were shocked, and we were hard put to explain.

When my mother heard of it, that I had made another change after only four years of service, she was very upset and wrote me a scathing letter. She gave me a dressing down the likes of which I had never had before--a Pope could not have done a better job. She knew how to quote the Bible--shepherds that take care of the sheep for the sake of the wool, etc. But that was my dear mother. To her, I was still the little boy who gambled away her grocery money at the marketplace. My defense was that I did it out of financial necessity, since I had to send them some money practically on a monthly basis. The additional salary would make things easier for me. But that explanation was unacceptable. She replied, "I would rather go hungry than be in part responsible for your leaving your flock."

Mother had only two masters--Jesus Christ and Martin Luther. She had Christ's compassion and Luther's stubbornness.

So, not having an enemy that we knew of in the church, our four years of happy ministry had come to an unexpected end. It was the first church we ever left without specific reason, and I always felt guilty about it.

## Chapter 19
## WAR YEARS IN PORTLAND, OREGON

IN MANY RESPECTS PORTLAND marked the climax of our ministry. The Second World War was in full progress. America had entered the war on the side of England and France, while at the same time fighting the Japanese in the Pacific. Zion had made its fair share of contributing young men to the armed forces. The bulletin hanging in the entrance hall displayed names and pictures of all the servicemen ranking from privates to captains. One of the youngest and last ones to be inducted made the first supreme sacrifice by going down with the ship *Liscom Bay* in the South Pacific.

Every Sunday evening service was dedicated to one of the men in the service. The name of the person to be remembered on a particular evening in thought and prayer, would be announced one week ahead of time. Letters that we received from the boys on the front were highly appreciative and touching. We received a letter from an anonymous writer, one which he had written prior to going into battle.

Dear Rev. Kalmbach:
Well, here it's Christmas, and I believe this is the first Christmas I have ever spent away from home. It don't seem like Christmas, but then I consider myself lucky to be alive and with at least a chance of again coming home.

Reverend, I have a poem that I would like to have you read in Christian Endeavor, because I believe it expresses a certain thought every serviceman has in his heart. If you don't think it wise, you can do with it what you please.

If I could find the proper words
    Or had the proper diction,
I could tell about a sweeter girl
    Than you read about in fiction.

I wouldn't say she is gorgeous,
    Or that she's sugar sweet.
These words are used too commonly
    To describe this girl of mine.

Even Webster could not help me,
    With all his knowledge to impart,
For there are no words he could use
    To describe the goodness in her heart.

Of all the girls I'll ever know,
    There'll never be another
To take the place in my heart
    Of you, my darling mother!

Needless to say, the Sunday night services were always attended to capacity.
  One of my most devoted and loyal workers among the young people was a cobbler by the name of David Brauer. One

could always depend on him to come up with an original idea to make the service interesting and meaningful.

There were always some heavy hearts that needed comforting. Never was there a time when my ministry was more meaningful. Sympathy and comfort came easier to me since I, too, was plagued by worry over my family in Russia.

Yes, in Zion the minister was kept busy. Besides the church work, certain demands were made upon my time by the General Conference. Aside from being president of the seminary school board, I had been given the job of writing the Sunday school lessons. These lessons had to be put out in pamphlet form every three months. The little extra income was appreciated and very much needed with demands from Russia ever increasing.

The church, like most of the German Congregational churches, had a strong prayer meeting group addicted to pietism. They always met twice a week, on Sunday afternoon and Wednesday night. The minister was always expected to attend. They had their own organization; it was sort of a church within the church. They had their elder, who would choose the speakers for the meeting. Some of these speakers had become quite eloquent. Often other brethren from the East or California would come to visit, which was always a special occasion. The other sister churches suspended their own meetings and always got together in the same place. Stating that some of the speakers had become eloquent also implies that some had become rabblerousers, causing people to fall on their knees, praying out loud sometimes, ten or more at one time.

According to my own concept of what the Christian faith should be, some of the action always seemed to be an anachronism. I could never feel quite comfortable. Despite the fact that some of the brethren were the backbone of the congregation, their emotionalism went against my nature. There was too much stress laid on punishment and retribution instead of love and compassion. The way some of them preached hell and damnation, one could almost smell the brimstone. I would sit there, thinking, Why would they not concentrate on revealing the love and compassion of God instead of presenting him as vindictive, jealous and vain? I could not help but speculate what some of these people would be if the fear of hell and damnation were eliminated. Would they be Christians for the sheer joy that a Christian life can bring?

As a rule, the minister was always the last one to be called upon. That way he would not be overshadowing the visiting orators and would be in position to summarize everything. Sometimes the minister had the unpleasant duty of correcting statements made by some zealous speaker. On one occasion, the speaker prophesied impending doom, and used as an illustration Jesus' weeping over Jerusalem and prophesying its destruction. The visiting evangelist was so carried away that he made the statement, "And do you know that that prophecy came true not too long after Christ's death, when the City of Jerusalem was completely destroyed by Alexander the Great." It put me somewhat in a predicament, and I knew that if called upon to make the closing remarks I could not let that statement go unchallenged. I complimented the brother for his sincerity and zeal but had to make a slight correction, namely that Alexander the Great lived over three hundred years before Christ. So obviously he could not have been the one who had destroyed Jerusalem. Some of the brethren criticized me for embarrassing the visitor, but one sister stepped up and said, "It serves him right. If he doesn't know what he is talking about, he should keep his mouth shut."

But despite everything, the prayer group made our church stronger.

Heretofore we were able to keep up correspondence with our people in Russia, but now all of a sudden the mail stopped.

The "butcher," Stalin, had decided that all German people living in Russia were potential traitors and enemies of the state, especially those in the Caucasus and south Ukraine district. These people had to be removed from the path of the advancing German army lest they join their kin and become traitors. He turned his NKVD (secret police) loose on these unfortunate people, whose only crime was that they had German blood. What horrors were perpetrated came to light after the war.

Worry and uncertainties caused me to have again sleepless nights and terrible nightmares. These nightmares always had the same characteristics. I came home to visit my people only to find my mother locked up in a dark room hopelessly insane. She was unable to recognize me. Amelia always had to shake me out of them; I was usually wringing wet.

One night I jumped out of bed. It startled Amelia, and she wanted to know what had happened. I asked her, "Couldn't you hear that gunshot? It was as if the explosion had happened right in our bedroom." She tried to assure me that it was just a bad dream. I protested that I had not had a dream; I had just heard the gunshot. The significance of that night's experience was revealed to us several months after the war, when my nephew came over from West Germany to pay us a visit.

Many Russian ships docked in Portland for repairs and cargo. One of our young men, who worked as a welder on these ships, suggested to me that since I was able to speak the Russian language I could get a job as an interpreter.

I had decided on moonlighting and went to work. The main reason I had made the decision was the hope that I might learn what had happened to our people. It was not easy to get the truth from any of them. They had been trained to conceal the truth. Luckily the way the Russians pronounced my name made it sound Ukrainian, and they kept insisting that I was a cossack who had escaped. No matter how much I denied it, they just did not believe me. One of them asked me where I had picked up the Russian language. When I told them that I had learned it in school, he laughed and said that he had never heard a foreigner who had learned the language speak with no accent.

I must have had a remarkable teacher, he said. There were even a couple of little boys on the ship who kept following me around and repeating the fact that I was a Russian cossack.

One day I managed to put a tricky question to one of the sailors, and he unwittingly gave me an answer I wanted to hear. I approached him with the remark, "With the German army advancing into southern Russia, you must have a good deal of trouble with the German people in the Caucasus, eh?" "Oh, no," he answered. "Most of them are not there anymore; they have been moved." He was careful not to say that they had been exiled.

There was one officer, the first mate, and a woman who gave me more information than any of them. She had been thoroughly disillusioned and told me more in detail what had happened. She also told me that while many believed that I was an escapee, she, on the other hand, believed that I was in the service of the American secret service. "Don't believe anything that the sailors tell you. They have been trained to spread false propaganda. The truth is that Russia, far from being a worker's paradise, is actually a slave state worse than that during the czar's time."

I was beginning to become apprehensive. Was this woman leading me on? A few nights later I got my answer.

About midnight someone rang the doorbell at the parsonage. When I opened the door, I faced this woman from the Russian ship. She was obviously very agitated and excitedly related the fact that she was defecting. She asked whether we could hide her. I refused to let her in the house, assuring her that it would be the first place they would look for her, and that I had no desire to become involved. But I did give her the advice that if she really was defecting, then the best thing for her to do would be to get out of town as fast as she could and head for San Francisco. There was a good-sized colony of Russians there; and I told her that they, no doubt, would be willing to give her protection.

As I suspected, the following morning, early, some of the ship's personnel came to see me and wanted to know whether I knew where she was. I volunteered to let them search the house if they liked. I said that she had come to see me but that I had refused to be of any help to her.

A few weeks later, after the ship had left Portland, I received an anonymous postcard from San Francisco: "I am safe. Thank you for the advice." Well, I knew that it could have come only from one person.

The two cabin boys who kept following me around approached me with a request. Would I take them in my car down to the city center? To get rid of them, I suggested that if the captain would give them permission, I would. I had, of course, no idea that the captain would grant them that wish. I was mistaken; they soon returned, all smiles, telling me what the captain had said: "If P.K. will take you, it will be all right." I was hooked. My trip with them was most interesting. They had all sorts of questions to ask me: "Do all your workers own their own homes? Do they own their own cars?" They observed and noticed everything.

When they saw a black man in uniform, they were surprised and commented, "We did not know you had black people in the armed service." I explained that according to the black population we had proportionately just as many if not more blacks in uniform. "Yes, but you will not let them serve alongside the white soldiers." They constantly made comparisons and pointed out where their system was superior. It was a propaganda trip in which I was to be brainwashed by a couple of children. The fact that these youngsters had so much information intrigued me. I enjoyed the trip very much.

Back on board ship, they expressed their gratitude and added teasingly: "We still think that you are a Kubansky cossack." They wanted to do something for me; so they brought me a couple of beginner's school textbooks, a first grade reader and one on grammar.

Paging through these books, it was easy

to see why they had so many questions.
From the very first lesson to the last page,
it was propaganda. Every lesson either
glorified some citizen who had distinguished himself as a Communist or condemned
one who was not living up to the rules. And
always shots were being taken at capitalism
or religion. The word *kulack* (protester)
appeared often. It meant that they were
people opposing and refusing to join the
*kulchos*, wanting to hold on to their
possessions and unwilling to share; they
were bad citizens. I quote one lesson as
an example:

> During the terrible hunger years
> when people were starving, they
> prayed to God for bread. God
> did not answer their prayers.
> Then the people turned to Lenin
> and asked him for bread, and our
> glorious leader gave them bread. A
> good Communist, therefore, does
> not believe in God but believes in
> his leaders.

Despite this thorough brainwashing and training, there were still some to be found who did their own thinking, for instance, a certain ship's cook. First making sure that no one could overhear him, he volunteered to do some adverse propagandizing: "You know, P.K., when I drive through your residential districts and see all those well-kept homes owned by your working class, I become very sad and just as soon would return home as quickly as I could so that I would not have to see all this. To see how things are done and how your people are treated by comparison to my people makes it hard for one to return home. We have as individuals no future other than just keeping alive. There is no ambition to get ahead. Your workers are happy at their work, and they do not have to keep watch over their shoulders for someone spying on them. They are really free!"

I had befriended a young captain who also had his home in the Caucasus. He often invited me to his cabin for some *zakuska* (a snack and vodka). He suggested that I write a letter to my mother. He said he would see to it that she got it. He was very sympathetic. During one of these visits he raised the question of a second front. "Why does not the U.S. open up a second front in Russia?" My answer was that we *had* opened up a second front. "If you had not received help and supplies from America, shipped to your armed forces, what could you have done to stop the Germans? While you were fighting we kept the trans-Siberian railroad busy hauling guns and ammunition."

"Yes," he answered, "but that makes it a cheap victory for you."

That remark stung me, and I made a reply that I soon wished that I had not made. Showing a bit of sarcasm, I answered, "True, we traded you the cheapest commodity we had, guns, for the cheapest you had--Russian blood."

That made my friend angry; it was the first time we had disagreed on something. I immediately apologized and explained that he should not blame me for having a bitter feeling. He accepted my apology and indicated that he could understand why I had made the remark.

One morning I was walking up the gangplank with a newspaper under my arm. The captain called to me. He wanted to know the latest news. I told him that the headlines stated that Stalin had abolished the Third International. While quoting the headline, I put my tongue in my cheek. He asked, "Don't you believe that?"

I countered with, "Do you? To abolish the Third International would mean giving up the Communist mission of spreading the system to other countries--that I cannot believe."

He, too, agreed that Stalin had made that announcement to please and satisfy Roosevelt, etc. There was rejoicing in the nation over the brave effort our ally Russia was making in order to crush Hitler. None could believe that the bear that had clawed Hitler to death would stop with that. While we were in the process of destroying one monster, we were cuddling another.

It was a great day when finally the war came to an end. The day the armistice was signed there was again singing and dancing in the streets. It was a repetition of what had happened after the First World War.

Our church held a special thanksgiving service. Broken families were again united, and the boys returned home from the front.

Some of the boys who just a short time ago had left home as mere boys now returned as men. Their experiences, as they related them, were spellbinding. War atrocities committed on both sides were attested to, none more horrible than those committed against the Jewish people. German concentration camps had become a stench in the nostrils of humanity. No one at the time had the least suspicion that the crimes against the Jews had been almost duplicated in crimes against the German people in Russia. In numbers of people murdered and exiled, Stalin had matched his cohort Hitler.

With the war over, things gradually went back to normal. I had great hopes of again being able to resume correspondence with my people. It had been almost two years since my last letter from mother. Mail service however, was not reestablished.

One day I received a telephone call from the Red Cross, inquiring whether the name Robert Belz had any meaning to me. When I told them that I had a nephew in Russia by that name, the lady answered that she had some good news; the party that had been trying to contact me was an escapee from Russia now living in West Germany, and that person had given them the name of his uncle in America. The fact that I was a minister made it fairly easy for the Red Cross to locate me. All they had to do was page through some church yearbooks.

I immediately wrote to Robert and had an answer within a short time. His letter broke my heart and put me on the verge of a nervous breakdown. He gave me a complete history of events that had taken place during the last war years. My mother had had to make the trip into exile at the age of eighty-two and had died on the way. His own father had been executed on trumped-up charges accusing him of committing sabotage. So had been my youngest sister, Rosalia, and her husband. His mother (my sister Maria) and sisters had been exiled to Kazakhstan.

The episode that broke my spirit more than any other was reading about the arrest and execution of Rosalia and her husband. They had lived in Southern Caucasus near the Black Sea. The police had come and dragged the parents away at midnight and had taken them to the police station for interrogation. Their two little innocent children, one four and the other six years old, never saw their parents again. I kept repeating to myself over and over again: How could God let that happen? Why they merited execution by a firing squad was a mystery to me. Perhaps Stalin feared that they would help the advancing Germany army.

The orphaned children were then adopted

by John and his kindly wife, Elena. They raised them with their own son, who by that time had already gained recognition as a fighter pilot.

It must be said in fairness to the Kruschev era that the government sent my sister and apology and completely exonerated her husband from any wrongdoing. He was an innocent victim of a jealous commissar.

Brother John did not fare quite so badly, no doubt because of the fact that he had in the early years of the revolution been active in the Social Democratic party, supporting the Kerensky government, and was merely considered one who had slightly different training. They let him choose his own point of exile as long as he gave them the assurance that he would never again return to the South. He moved to a city north of Moscow.

As far as I was concerned, the distressing news caused me to be despondent. The vampire bats of doubt were again descending upon me. It became almost impossible for me to preach. How could

God be considered love and let such horrible injustice and cruelty fall upon innocent little children?

In the quiet solitude of my study I did some intense soul-searching. How could I continue in the ministry, bringing solace and comfort to others, while unable to comfort myself? Words kept sticking in my throat, and I often broke out into tears. I felt it would be unfair to the congregation to subject them every Sunday to a display of confused emotions. I had to resign!

Would my leaving the church be considered or interpreted as desertion or unfaithfulness? That must not be. Even Jesus had his moments of doubt and despair. Why else would he have called out, "My God, my God, why hast thou forsaken me?"

As it was only a temporary crisis with him, so I must have time to think and somehow try to rebuild my crumbled faith. I could not give up God, for every tree, every flower and blade of grass, the stars, the sky, all testify as to his existence. "The heavens declare the glory of God."

But as my father in years past rebuilt his mill and caused a superior building to rise out of the rubble, so I must rebuild my faith, even though giving up some handed-down traditions and concepts. It would not be rebuilt according to the blueprint of the Old Testament, but would be created entirely around the concept of Christ with the emphasis on *building character*. The creation of hell or heaven on earth does not rest with God, but with man. By adhering to that philosophy of life, I would be able to believe what Meister Eckhardt said: "The fleetest beast to bear one to perfection is suffering." That there is so much suffering caused by man's inhumanity to man is not God's fault; the responsibility and blame must rest squarely on man's shoulders.

Out walking one day, deep in thought, trying to put things in their places, I stepped over a worm that was trying to make his way across the sidewalk. Without thinking, I turned, picked up the worm, and laid him on safe ground. After I had gone a few steps, the thought came to me: Why did I pick up that worm? There is no doubt that during my lifetime I had stepped on many a worm without ever showing concern. And the more I thought about it, the more the whole act became symbolic. Maybe that is the entire secret of a happy and successful life: to condense the whole purpose and aspirations into a word that has the same number of letters as love, namely, *care*. Care for one another; care for other living things. *It is the key to decency, compassion, and love.*

It took an insignificant worm to bring my thinking to the right path and show me the purpose of life. Why spin fantastic tales of a hereafter? The practical life here upon earth is all one needs to worry about. Whether there is a paradise or hell beyond the grave, paradise will rightly come to him who has fulfilled his obligations on earth by caring. To live a life of compassion will most certainly bring one in tune with the golden rule: "Love thy neighbor as thyself."

Care would do away with ammunitions factories and armament plants. It would induce scientists to put their efforts in making nuclear power improve life upon earth, and not compete to bring about the most devastating implements of murder and destruction. It would bring about a society in which the poorest pauper could receive the same medical attention as the rich man. Yes, even where a poor man could afford to die and have a decent burial.

A pool of water freshly created by rainfall will soon evaporate and again descend upon the thirsty petals of a rose. If it does not spend itself, it will become an evil-smelling pesthole spreading disease. Unless one has a church within one's own heart from where to draw the strength for an abundant life, all praying and wailing will be of no consequence, but merely will reveal hypocrisy.

But now to return to my decision to give up the ministry. When I discussed my intentions with Amelia, and told her that is was also my doctor's advice that I should get away from tension and stress, she was in total agreement.

After I had resigned, I was approached by

one of the deacons, who told me that the church would be willing to raise my salary by a considerable amount if I would stay. I had to tell him that the salary had nothing to do with my decision, that my intention was to get away from the mental anguish caused by the destruction of my family in Russia, that I had to have some time to think. With my mental and emotional condition, I felt unable to bring any kind of message to other people as long as I found myself in confusion.

With a heavy heart, I delivered my farewell sermon. It really was not a sermon but more of an acknowledgment and thanks for the peaceful and cooperative spirit that the people had shown through my seven years of service. In conclusion, I asked the people to forgive me if on that Sunday morning they did not see me standing at the exit shaking hands with everybody. Mumbling a half-audible "Good-bye, and God bless you," I descended from the chancel. It would take some time for Amelia and the children to come home; so I hurried back to the parsonage to regain my composure, for I did not want my children to see their father sob like a little child. It was the most drastic and difficult decision I had ever made.

During the time I was moonlighting on the waterfront, we were able to save a few dollars. Loretta was attending Lewis and Clark College, and it was up to me to find the kind of work that would make it possible for her to continue and also make it possible for Dorothy, who was in her senior year in high school, to go to college.

As I was scanning the ad section looking for a suitable residence, I noticed a marked discrepancy in prices that, according to my observation, was not justified. There were homes that looked equal in every way except in price.

We reasoned, Why not buy a home that was in a rundown condition, fix it up, and resell it again at a higher price? The first home we bought we had reconditioned within a week. Before the second week was up we had sold it at a considerable profit.

So, accidentally, we had stumbled on a vocation that would feed and provide for the family. I used to refer to my newfound profession as one where I sold "tangible" homes instead of "intangible" ones.

Eventually the real estate broker through whom we bought and sold quite a few homes persuaded me to join his firm and sell on commission. Selling came natural to me, although my boss often remarked that even as a salesman I would never get over the preacher complex. Grounds for such a conclusion came to him when he overheard me talk a young couple out of buying an expensive home and then talk them into going for a much cheaper one. The boss's comment: "You are still a preacher at heart. Whoever heard of turning down a sale that would have meant a much higher commission in favor of one that was far less?"

Persuading the newlyweds not to go too heavily into debt resulted in selling to them and for them several times thereafter. They showed their gratitude for the service I had rendered. Too high monthly payments could very easily have caused tension and disagreement in their young lives.

The Million Dollar Club, a club admitting only ace salesmen, asked me to become a member.

The girls were both doing well in school. Dorothy, too, was now a college student attending Portland University and studying to become a nurse. She stayed at the hospital dormitory, while Loretta commuted by bus every day.

For a time we were worried about Loretta. Her school activities sometimes kept her away until midnight. The neighborhood where we resided did not help our peace of mind. Despite our repeated warnings of danger, she still was unafraid. I decided to give her a lesson and a scare she was not likely to forget.

One night, about midnight, I went down to the bus stop, hid behind a building, and waited for her. The bus finally arrived, and I saw her get off and start walking toward home. Starting to walk a distance behind her, I made sure she would hear my footsteps. Knowing that someone was following her, she started to increase her speed--and so did I. By the time I had reached the corner of the street on which was our home, she was nowhere to be seen. Apparently, after turning the corner, she had put on an Olympic sprint. As I reached the house, I noticed her parting the curtains and peeking to get a glimpse of her follower. She was still practically out of breath when I entered the house. She gasped, "Dad, was that you following me? You could have given me a heart attack!" I felt a bit ashamed and apologized. I was sorry. But the experience she had had resembled what could have happened. She never forgot it, and made it a point to come home earlier from then on.

The life in real estate agreed with me. My health had improved, and I really felt as if years had been taken from my age. Occasionally someone would say to me, "We know that you gave up the ministry to get away from tension. Isn't real estate just as nerve-racking?" My answer was that I did not let it bother me, And I never lost any sleep over the success of failure of the day.

My latest project now was to get my nephew to come to America and possibly get him to stay here. He agreed to come.

In the meantime, Amelia made several trips to the Midwest to see some of her relatives that she had not seen for a long while. When she returned from visiting her sister in Milwaukie, Wisconsin she had some fantastic rumors to relate about her husband, who had become a "turncoat" and had left the ministry to chase the dollar. The rumors were that I had become a playboy, that I had become an alcoholic, that I had become a gambler.

It was thought that I had become a playboy because I was not attending church and enjoyed going out to parties.

They thought I was an alcoholic because I had joined the German Aid Society, and the men got together once a week for a social evening of singing, and, of course, in connection with the evening's activities, a glass of beer.

And they thought I was a gambler because a friend from one of our former churches paid us a visit and took us to a horse race. Unfortunately, the man checking our entrance tickets was a member of one of the sister churches and lost no time in spreading the rumor that I was a "horse player." This latest conclusion was strengthened by an episode that happened at a carnival that the society put on in order to raise money for an old people's home. One of the means by which money was raised for the old people's home was a bingo game. The lady who called out the numbers suddenly fell ill and wanted to be relieved of her job. Amelia and I were sitting on a bench nearby. One of the members came over and asked whether I would be kind enough to take her place. I consented, of course. That had made me a gambler. Again one of the church members of a sister church had witnessed the terrible spectacle and had to report how low that ex-minister had fallen.

I attended a church conference held in the city in order to see old friends. One of the roaming lay evangelists approached me and whispered to me out of the side of his mouth, "I hear you sold out," meaning that I had turned my back on the church. I told him I had not sold out; I had merely turned the stone over to someone else. The man reminded me of some character out of Aesop's Fables. So instead of getting angry at him, I was reminded of what the German poet Schiller had said: "Against ignorance and stupidity even the gods fight in vain."

It was again time for Amelia to take another trip to see her relatives. This time the stories regarding her wayward husband were of entirely different nature but equally incredible. Instead of referring to me now as a fallen minister, they suddenly elevated me to the status of a millionaire. Again someone had seen a picture of me in the newspaper, mentioning the fact that an ex-minister had made good in real estate and was a charter member of the Million Dollar Club. Now, that word *million* was all that had to be mentioned. The fact that anyone selling about $250,000 worth of real estate could qualify did not mean anything to someone who liked to exaggerate and spread gossip; to him the minister who had left the church for financial reasons had now become a millionaire. How ridiculous people can be! By this time we were used to rumors and would not let any gossip or outright lying change our lives in any way.

Both our daughters had graduated from college and had established themselves in their chosen professions. Loretta went into teaching, and Dorothy into nursing. Dorothy was the first to get married. Two years later Amelia and I experienced the greatest joy that can come to any parent, the birth of the first grandchild. As a parent, one naturally plays the part of a disciplinarian. Children must be directed and guided, and that sometimes requires disciplinary action. But a grandparent does not have to do those unpleasant tasks. Grandpa and grandma just can sit back and play the part of spoilers. It is a wonderful experience but does not *always* produce the best results.

We were now looking forward to the

nephew's visit from Germany. He had arrived in New York and notified us as to the date of his arrival in Portland.

On the long-awaited date Amelia and I drove to the station to meet him.

## Chapter 20
## THE NEPHEW HAS ARRIVED

WE WERE ALL ANXIOUS TO MEET my nephew, whom I had never seen and who was born after I had left Russia. He would now personally bring us all the details of what had gone on in Russia.

On the day of his arrival, Amelia and I went to the station to meet him. The train pulled in, and we stationed ourselves as close as we could to the exit of the coach. I kept peering in through the window in hopes that I would be able to recognize him. When he came to the steps and I got a full view of him, there was no guessing--he looked just like his father, who was also my village playmate. He likewise had no difficulty in recognizing his uncle, since, according to him, I looked just like my mother. We went towards each other with extended arms. We embraced each other for a while in silence; then, when I looked around to introduce him to his aunt, we saw Amelia standing there with tears in her eyes.

Early childhood malnutrition had definitely left its mark upon his physical appearance. He looked and acted as a man who had come out of purgatory. It was hard for him to smile. One got the impression that the young man considered it almost sacrilegious to show joy. We felt very sorry for him. To minimize one's own sorrow, one has to look at someone with even greater sorrow.

We tried very hard to cheer him up, being careful not to dig into his past before he himself was ready to tell us.

When he finally started to relate past events in Russia, there was no stopping him. I shall here let him tell his story.

"Uncle if it had not been for the food packages you kept sending us, I would not be here today. Mother had to walk miles to the station in order to pick them up, but they saved our lives."

At this point my mind went back to the time when my sister Maria reprimanded mother for sending her son to America. Here was proof that Providence had had a hand in my destiny. Listening to him was like watching a moving film.

He continued: "Whenever we received food, we had to hide it very carefully in order not to have it stolen. Children constantly cried for food."

Here again I remembered a letter from Rosalia telling me of her two little ones' constantly being hungry and saying, "Mama, we just ate. Why are we still hungry?"

Every once in a while his narrative was interrupted for a moment of silence as he struggled to control his emotions before continuing: "The government edict that all property had to be turned into the *kolchos* worsened their life in the village, and they became desperate. Those that offered protest were uprooted and sent elsewhere. Some were sent to the southern Caucasus below the city of Tiblisy, and still others farther on to Kazakhstan. Our family was permitted to stay because the government thought they could use my father as a sort of foreman in the *kolchos* assisting the appointed commissar. But the commissar seemed to take a dislike to father. It was no doubt jealousy, since people went for advice to father more often than to him. He was an ill-tempered Georgian and had no love for German people."

He came now to the episode for which I was waiting with baited breath, and I was almost afraid to listen: the arrest and death of Rosalia and her husband.

"Aunt Rosalia and her husband, with their two little daughters, lived in a town near the Black Sea. Her husband was an electrical engineer, she, a bookkeeper. It was during the time that the Germans were coming ever closer to the Caucasus. Stalin and his henchman, the dog Barea, invoked a period of terror. Both Rosalia and her husband were removed from the family and executed unbeknownst to the sleeping children, who next morning found their parents missing. The news that Aunt Rosalia and her husband had been killed struck terror into the hearts of all of us, and we did not know who would be next."

For obvious reasons Robert kept the story of his father's death and the tragedy that had befallen his own family for last.

"Greatgrandfather had been fortunate enough to die during the early part of the revolution. The property was inherited by his eldest son, my grandfather, and during the last years had been occupied by my own family. During our time the property also was taken into the collective system. We had to move into the bunkhouse, and the estate house was turned into a hospital. We were a family of four--my three sisters ranged in age between eleven and sixteen. I had been in Krasnodar attending a business school and had returned home for the summer prior to seeking a position somewhere. Father and I were in the process of hitching up a team to drive out into the field to check on the workers.

"Through the front gate appeared a group of mounted uniformed men recognizable as the Russian secret police. They were led by the commissar. The leader of the group aproached father and barked out, 'Comrade Belz, you are under arrest. You have been charged with blowing up a bridge behind the retreating Russian army.' When father asked for specifics concerning how that sabotage was supposed to have been accomplished, their answer was that he used dynamite, which fact the commissar corroborated. Of course, father then realized that it was all the commissar's doing and there was no more need to protest. The only hope, which was very little, lay in proving to the magistrate that the charges were false.

"The scene had attracted the attention of my mother and my sister. They stood in front of the door, watching. When the police started to drag father away, mother and sister started to weep and begged the men to release father. They would not. Father had only enough time to say to me, "Don't worry, Son. I am not guilty and will soon be home again. In the meantime, the family is yours to take care of." With that we saw father led away to the nearest prison compound, which was about ten miles from our home.

"The day after the arrest I took a trip to the *stanitza* in hopes of getting a glimpse of father and maybe having a few words with him. We still did not realize how serious the matter actually was. I reached the stockade and saw prisoners walking around behind a high mesh fence with several strands of barbed wire strung along the top. I was looking for father. I saw him just coming out of one of the buildings. Fortunately, he saw me, too. He approached one of the guards and pointed in my direction, apparently telling the guard that I was his son, and asking for permission to have a few words with me. The guard nodded, and father came over to talk to me. He waved for me to come closer and turned sideways so that I could see his back as he partially pulled up his shirt. They had beaten him the night before. I could now understand why he had that peculiar walk as he approached me--it was as if he were bending back his shoulders to keep his shirt from touching his back, which had been cut to ribbons. Father told me that he was permitted only a few minutes, and he only wanted to repeat to me that the family was now my concern. He was now certain that he would never be able to return to his family. Despite the fact that they could not beat a confession out of him, they nevertheless were not going to admit that they had made a mistake--life was cheap.

"Father also told me that he was sure the commissar himself had blown up the bridge just to frame father. He also told me that he had overheard a conversation to the effect that the rest of the villagers were soon to be exiled. The village was in the direct path on the oncoming German army and had to be vacated.

"The guard who had given permission for our short visit now signaled that our time was up. Father hurriedly once more told me to tell the family that he loved them, but things were now in God's hands and we must not lose faith. It was the last time I ever saw my father.

"Going back home, I felt utterly crushed. How could I break the news to the family that their father was doomed? I was now also overcome with consuming hate for that lying animal and decided on revenge if at all possible. I would even the score with that man no matter how long it took.

"Within a few weeks, the rest of the villagers received their orders to get ready to relocate. The destination this time was Kazakhstan, in the Siberian district. The order came as no surprise; they had been expecting it. To make things worse for some of the families, the young men near military age would have to stay back. They would shortly be inducted into the labor battalion and sent to the front to dig trenches and erect fortifications.

"We were herded into a freight car and kept behind locked doors for two days. Among the group was my good friend Benjamin, who family had suffered a like fate. We agreed that we would always stay close to one another. The work assigned to us was northwest of Rostov on the Don. The German army was driving towards Rostov, their next objective. The Russian army was in flight and had moved to Rostov to make a stand. For a while it looked as if the Germans would be driven back, but they received reinforcements and eventually prevailed. My friend Ben and I, with hearts full of hate, felt no loyalty to our homeland, and decided to let ourselves be captured. Better to wait out the war in a prison camp than to fight for a nation unworthy of loyalty.

"One day some of the Germans appeared behind us. We held up our hands and walked toward them, calling to them that we were Germans. We were led into the officers' quarters for interrogation. After we had told them our story, we asked them whether they could possibly use us as scouts, since we knew the ountry and the army was heading towards our home district. The officers agreed.

"We had to take a crash course in

handling a motorcycle with a sidecar. We were each issued a machine gun and assigned to scouting duty. The army was now headed in the direction of Krasnodar. Ben and I were rejoicing, for that could possibly bring us near our village. Our hopes of meeting our friend the commissar rose high. Within a short time we were past Krasnodar and turning southward into the Caucasus. We had come closer to our village. Ben and I went to see our German captain. After we had told him of our past experience, we asked him for permission to visit the village. The village was now a German occupied zone, and we did not have to be afraid. Realizing what had been in our minds, the captain consented and granted us that favor.

"Ben was in control of the motorcycle. I, with the gun across my lap, sat in the sidecar. We roared into the village. We recognized no one. The new inhabitants were a conglomerate of Georgians, Russians and Mongols. We stopped to ask whether the commissar was still in charge. They pointed out his living quarters to us. We knocked at his door. The half-dressed commissar came to the door. It did not take him long to recognize his former village boys-- now in German uniform. He turned pale but invited us in, pretending calmness and hospitality. Guessing our possible motive for looking him up, he commenced to apologize for the tragic events that had taken place and tried to convey the impression that he had been forced to give false testimony to frame our fathers. We told him why we had come to see him and informed him that he had ten minutes left. He started to beg for mercy, even went down on his knees. It was rather ironic that the man who could boldly look on when innocent people were shot down would now himself ask for mercy. I answered him that we would give him the same kind of mercy that he had given my father. After the ten minutes were up, that evil brain that concocted so many lies to send people to their deaths was no more in a condition to do any more harm--it was splattered across the dining table.

"Ben stepped on the starter, and we roared out of the village to join our company. We still had nothing but hate in our hearts, but the terrible gnawing for revenge was gone, and that at least was a relief."

When Robert had finished the tragic episode, the thought occurred to me to ask him the approximate date of Rosalia's execution. When he told us, Amelia gave a gasp. Putting her hand over her mouth, she said, "My God! That was the time you jumped out of bed claiming that you heard a gunshot!"

When it was explained to Robert what had happened, he nodded his head and said, "Uncle, you have inherited your mother's intuition."

"Yes," Amelia agreed. "He sometimes scares me with his intuitions."

By this time Robert had sufficiently composed himself to go on with the narrative. "Due to the disastrous outcome of the Stalingrad battle, we were ordered to retreat. The Russians had completely routed the Germans and captured their Field Marshal Von Paulus. The war in Russia was practically over.

"Within a few weeks we found ourselves in Germany and ordered to the southern front to face the Americans. It was already common knowledge that Germany had lost the war. The only question everybody asked was, What would happen to Berlin? Would the Allies permit the Russians to take it? Some of the German officers contacted some of the American officers and promised to join their men, the Americans marching on Berlin, in order to get there before the Russians did. The Americans refused the help. These German officers broke down and cried. It was obvious to them that the Russians had been given the green light. The Russians were given a free hand, and what they did is history."

We tried everything we could to bring Robert out of his depressed mood, but nothing worked. I said to my wife, that if we could break through that shell he had built around himself and get him to laugh once, maybe we could get somewhere.

We decided to take him with our family, including Loretta and Dorothy, over to the coast of Seaside; it would probably help to relieve the tension.

As we were driving along, reminiscing about Russia, we accidentally drove past a stop sign. A policeman saw it and came after us with his siren going. In lieu of a cussword, I used an old German village swear word quite commonly used. But since he had not heard that for so long, it struck Robert funny. He started to laugh almost hysterically. It was as if all of a sudden the dam he had built so many years ago had broken down. He said, laughing, "I haven't heard that word since I left home." From that moment on, he was a different man. The officer stopped us and merely gave us a warning not to drive past stop signs.

After returning from the beach, Robert insisted on finding a job. I went along with him and got him located in one of the local furniture factories. He stayed with us for the entire summer, but it became increasingly obvious that he was homesick for Europe. He knew that his mother and sisters were still alive and thought that he should at least make an effort to be as near them as possible in the event they, too, might join him in West Germany.

When he had saved enough money for his return trip, he made his wish known. He wanted to go back to Germany. Nothing could dissuade him.

During the last few years we have been keeping in touch with him. He had a family and is a successful furniture merchant in West Germany.

His mother recently passed away; so he, too, had never been able to see his mother again. He had had a letter from his sister just prior to his mother's death, in which she had told him that during Krushchev's time their mother had received documentation from the Soviet government completely exonerating their father. Robert also informed us that out of the eleven nephews and nieces still in Russia, five of them were doctors and three, teachers. It is rather ironic that a government that could be so ruthless with one generation could give so much attention to the next. Presumably it takes martyr's blood to fertilize the soil for future generations.

## Chapter 21
# LIFE IN ITS GREATEST DIMENSION

NOW, AT THE AGE OF SEVENTY-NINE, as the sunset of my life approaches, and I sit in my study enveloped by nostalgia, I find that time had been a clever bookkeeper. It has managed to hide and obscure the unpleasant memories, leaving a balance of joyous and happy memories that overshadows everything.

In my wonderful family, daughters as well as grandchildren, I see my life's reward. Parents are happy at the advent of their children, but the real exalted dimension added to one's life comes with the appearance of grandchildren.

Loretta presented us with two lovely and bright granddaughters; Dorothy gave us one grandson and three granddaughters. Every one has been instrumental in compensating for every tear shed in the past. What a joy it was to see them storming into our home, shouting. "Grandma, have you got some chicken noodle soup?" There was nothing in our life more inspiring than to see the grandchildren growing up. They all worshiped their grandma, and she in turn worshiped them. As for me, I was glad to sit back and be second choice, for they were her life.

Amelia's ability to handle schoolchildren and her own was outstanding, but when it came to handling her grandchildren, she had no equal. She had a little blue notebook especially for recording the children's bright and innocent remarks. One could always see her searching for a pencil to record the latest gem coming from one of them between the ages of two and five.

When a three-year-old climbed over the fence, ripping her panties, and said, "Oh-oh! I sprung a leak!", that had to be recorded.

When the boy, at four, was flying a kite with a piece of paper tied to the string and was asked the reason for the note, he answered, "I am sending a letter to Jesus."

That she could not pass up.

One day, when one of the girls had done something naughty and grandma had reprimanded the little one, saying, "What you just did made the angels weep and the devil laugh," the little one stuck out her chin and answered, "Yes, but the devil looked around the corner and said, 'Atta girl!'," that had to be recorded.

Noticing one mixing a concoction of flour, molasses, and sugar, Dorothy once asked, "Honey, why are you making such a mess?" The answer came back, "I am making poison to kill outsects." Now, that was logical because if bugs that were in the house were called *in*sects, the one outdoors had to be *out*sects. That was too good not to record; it had to go into grandma's little book.

The last one, only three years old, was once seen taking a couple of eggs out of her mother's refrigerator. Her mother, curious about what the child was up to, kept watching her through the window. She observed that the eggs were placed in an old robin's nest that had fallen off a tree, and covered with fertilizer. The mother opened the window and called out, "What are you doing?" Back came a very indignant answer: "Well, you have to fertilize eggs if you want chickies." One can see how that would make grandma run for her pencil and blue book.

Doing some painting outside, I was observed by one of Loretta's girls, likewise less than four years old. Carrying a stepladder on my shoulder, I heard her shouting through the window: "Grandpa, you look like Jesus!" Now, these are just samples that would make one relegate one's own unhappy experiences to obscurity.

But as happens so often, after sunshine often comes clouds and even storms. This we had to experience when suddenly our roller coaster plunged from the pinnacle of exaltation to the very depths of sorrow. Grandma became ill. The doctor's diagnosis was that she had cancer. To me it was the pronouncement of a death sentence. The condition had advanced so far that an operation was not advised since the cancer had spread through her system. After prolonged and terrible suffering she passed on, bringing down a cloud of sadness not only on her own family but on the many children who needed her. For example, there was a little boy who lived two blocks away from us. After grandma was buried, this little fellow, who so often had come to visit her and had spent long hours with her on our back patio, came to the door and asked to see grandma. When I told him that grandma was not living here anymore, and that she had gone to heaven, he did not take my word for it and insisted on seeing for himself. Going to every room in our house, he kept calling for grandma. Satisfied that she was not home, he stomped out of the house, apparently angry. I had a For Sale sign on the lawn; and as he passed the sign, I saw him suddenly stop, pull up the sign, and throw it in the middle of the street. He no doubt blamed me for grandma's absence.

Yes, she was every child's grandmother. No wonder one of them, flying home with her parents on an airplane, kept looking for grandma up in the sky, and feeling very sad because grandma did not show herself.

I am thankful and happy that I have not reached the point of uselessness. I find a lot of things to do for my daughters, and I consider myself a handyman. I was also fortunate enough to acquire the hobby of landscape painting. Several of my pictures have been sold, and many others decorate the houses of my relatives.

If I had to live my life again and were back in Russia, knowing what I know now, and someone stepped up to me, handed me a sum of money, and said "This sum of money is to pay for your passage to anyplace in the world that you would like to live and spend the rest of your life," I would step up to the ticket window and say loud and clear, "A ticket to the United States of America." Despite some regrettable incidents in our democracy, America is still the greatest country in the world.

It does not concern me that I have not amassed great wealth or achieved any kind of fame to be recorded. The greatest reward of my life is the knowledge and assurance that after my demise my family will remember me as a good father and grandfather and others that knew me will say, "He was a decent human being."

Glossary of Russian Terms and Phrases

*balalaika* Russian stringed-instrument, similar to guitar and mandolin
*Bohaty Nemzy* the rich Germans
*bozcscar* fire
*bueble* little boy
*buika* wolfhound
*cossack* Russian soldier who carried bayonet or sword
*droshka* Russian produce wagon cart
*fatz* son?
*Gimnasium* college
*kolchos* collective farm
*komissar* overseer, police chief, constable, ruler of the village
*Krasnaya Uliza* Red Street
*kulack* people in Soviet Russia who refused to give up their farm for collective farming, protester
*kwass* popular beverage made of fermented bread crusts
*lapty* burlap
*nahaikas* riding whips with little lead balls at the end
*Posholl won*! Be gone!
*Potyomking* a Russian cruiser ship of the era famous due to a mutiny
*prainiky* cookies
*schultz* magistrate
*schwarz augiger* Daddy's black-eyed one
*shabban* sheep rancher
*sodzky* town marshal
*stanitza* small Russian community within village
*trackteer* restaurant of an inn
*troch!* Bingo!
*troika* Russian coach and hitched (often 2-horse) team
*trosha* wagon often workers/peasants used for sleeping
*zakuska* a snack and vodka
*Zar daloy* "Down with the Czar!"

www.ingramcontent.com/pod-product-compliance
Lightning Source LLC
Chambersburg PA
CBHW060937230426
43665CB00015B/1980